Lessons from Four Ancient Chinese Sages of Daoism and Confucianism

Written and Translated By
Thomas Hayes & 李思瑾 Li Sijin

First Published in Great Britain 2022 by Mirador Publishing

Copyright © 2022 by Thomas Hayes and Li Sijin

All rights reserved. No part of this publication may be reproduced or transmitted, in any form or by any means, without permission of the publishers or author excepting brief quotes used in reviews.

First edition: 2022

A copy of this work is available through the British Library.

ISBN: 978-1-914965-61-6

Mirador Publishing
10 Greenbrook Terrace
Taunton
Somerset
TA1 1UT

Acknowledgements

We are once again most grateful to Sarah and her team at Mirador Publishing. They have worked quickly and efficiently in the publishing of this book. They have been both flexible and courteous, acting with tenacity and good grace at all times.

We also wish to thank 周丰堇 Zhou Fengji, a professor of philosophy at Xiangtan University, Hunan province for his kind and considerate checking of the original sourced Chinese language.

About the Authors

Thomas Hayes

THOMAS HAYES HAS STUDIED and practised the Daoist Arts for more than thirty-five years. In addition to practising Chen style meditation, taijiquan and qigong, he also studies the Yì Jīng and other associated Chinese Daoist and Buddhist metaphysical systems. He has also cultivated under other Buddhist, Advaita Vedanta, and Yoga traditions. He has qualifications in Stress Management, Life Coaching, Hypnotherapy and NLP. He is also a qualified TEFL teacher.

He works as a Data Protection and Cyber Security Consultant and is a Fellow of both the British Computer Society and the International Association of Privacy Professionals. He is certified by the UK's National Cyber Security Centre (NCSC) as an approved Cyber Security Consultant. He is a registered British Computer Society Examiner in advanced database design. He also provides help and advice in promoting Chinese and UK cultural exchanges. He lives in Manchester, England.

This is his fourth collaborative book. His first, *Chen Tàijíquán: The Theory and Practice of a Daoist Internal Martial Art: Volume 1 – Basics and Short Form* was written with Master Wang Hai Jun.

His second, *Qi Baishi: An Introduction to His Life and Art: The Artist Who Is as Highly Regarded by the Chinese as Picasso Is in the West* was also written with Li Sijin and published by Mirador Publishing in 2017. The third book, The Dao de Jing was published in 2020.

李思瑾 Li Sijin

李思瑾 Li Sijin has worked as an expert at the Qi Baishi Memorial

Hall in her hometown of Xiangtan City, Hunan, for the last twelve years. She has undertaken the detailed translation of the subject with Thomas Hayes, her previous co-author of Qi Baishi. She has injected much needed effort and a commensurate enthusiasm into the production of this book. She lives and breathes the Daoist philosophy.

She is also a practising accountant and an MC, hence she is a woman of wide-ranging skills and talent. She is especially interested in promoting the works of Qi Baishi and traditional Chinese culture in general to a Western audience.

Table of Contents

INTRODUCTION 1

SECTION 1 – CONFUCIUS 3

   ABOUT CONFUCIUS 3
   CHAPTER ONE 10
   CHAPTER TWO 15
   CHAPTER THREE 19
   CHAPTER FOUR 24
   CHAPTER FIVE 28
   CHAPTER SIX 35
   CHAPTER SEVEN 40
   CHAPTER EIGHT 44
   CHAPTER NINE 50
   CHAPTER TEN 54

SECTION 2 – MENCIUS 58

   ABOUT MENCIUS 58
   CHAPTER ELEVEN 61
   CHAPTER TWELVE 65
   CHAPTER THIRTEEN 67
   CHAPTER FOURTEEN 71
   CHAPTER FIFTEEN 75
   CHAPTER SIXTEEN 79
   CHAPTER SEVENTEEN 81
   CHAPTER EIGHTEEN 85

SECTION 3 – LAO ZI 89

   ABOUT LAO ZI 89
   CHAPTER NINETEEN 93
   CHAPTER TWENTY 97
   CHAPTER TWENTY-ONE 101
   CHAPTER TWENTY-TWO 105
   CHAPTER TWENTY-THREE 109
   CHAPTER TWENTY-FOUR 113
   CHAPTER TWENTY-FIVE 117
   CHAPTER TWENTY-SIX 121

SECTION 4 – ZHUANG ZI **124**

   ABOUT ZHUANG ZI 124
   CHAPTER TWENTY-SEVEN 126
   CHAPTER TWENTY-EIGHT 128
   CHAPTER TWENTY-NINE 130
   CHAPTER THIRTY 132

CHAPTER THIRTY-ONE	136
CHAPTER THIRTY-TWO	138
CHAPTER THIRTY-THREE	140
CHAPTER THIRTY-FOUR	142
CHAPTER THIRTY-FIVE	144
CHAPTER THIRTY-SIX	146
CHAPTER THIRTY-SEVEN	150
CHAPTER THIRTY-EIGHT	152
CHAPTER THIRTY-NINE	156
CHAPTER FORTY	158
CHAPTER FORTY-ONE	160
CHAPTER FORTY-TWO	162
CHAPTER FORTY-THREE	164
CHAPTER FORTY-FOUR	166
CHAPTER FORTY-FIVE	168
CHAPTER FORTY-SIX	170
CHAPTER FORTY-SEVEN	172
CHAPTER FORTY-EIGHT	174
CHAPTER FORTY-NINE	176
CHAPTER FIFTY	178
CHAPTER FIFTY-ONE	180
CHAPTER FIFTY-TWO	182
CHAPTER FIFTY-THREE	186
CHAPTER FIFTY-FOUR	188
CHAPTER FIFTY-FIVE	192
CHAPTER FIFTY-SIX	194
CHAPTER FIFTY-SEVEN	198
CHAPTER FIFTY-EIGHT	200
CHAPTER FIFTY-NINE	204
CHAPTER SIXTY	206

Introduction

TODAY IS CHRISTMAS DAY, 2021. A time for joy, reflection and, for some, the celebration of a spiritual teaching, Christianity. Yet, these celebrations are marred by restrictions on personal freedoms due to impositions by the state in response to Covid. These may be viewed either as paternalistic or sinister, depending on your view of those who rule over you.

The relationship between the ruled and the rulers is set out in the tales from the four ancient Chinese sages covered in this book. You must make up your own mind how well those who govern you meet their standards and equally how you may react to this.

There are four sages covered, two each from the two different traditions of Daoism and Confucianism. In this book we provide examples of stories and advice from all four sages. Both of these philosophies developed over the millennia into religions, forms of government and, alas, have been misappropriated for more sinister forms of governance and despotism. Daoism, especially, has produced various schools, religious institutions, martial arts, meditation, astrology, and art, and has influenced other religions, for example, Zen Buddhism.

The intention of the authors is not to provide a historical or metaphysical analysis but is merely to introduce these sages to an audience that may hitherto be totally or partially unfamiliar with them. Nor do we intend to provide a comparison of the two philosophies of Daoism and Confucianism.

The two sages covered as examples of Confucian philosophy are Kong Zi, known as Confucius in the West, and Meng Zi, known as Mencius. Zhuang Zi and Lao Zi are included as examples of the original Daoist thinkers.

As always with our combined efforts, we have produced this book from the original sources in the Chinese language and translated these into English. It is a difficult job to translate from ancient Chinese, especially when the text is in a form that is a combination of parable, fable, allegory, and metaphor. Just translating from modern Chinese to English can be somewhat complex.

We hope that, with our endeavours, we have achieved the correct balance, albeit that it may be judged that some of the content may well read as somewhat anachronistic. This is an obvious outcome if we are not to lose some of the poetry of the original language.

For those who wish to read more about Lao Zi and his famous Dao de Jing, we have produced an earlier book, also published by Mirador.

We hope that you can find some encouragement and understanding of human nature, society, and government in these troubling times.

SECTION 1 – CONFUCIUS

About Confucius

THE INDIAN (NEPALESE) BUDDHA, THE Chinese Confucius and the Greek Socrates are all examples of sages from antiquity. The Buddha sought to free believers all over the world from their suffering and to open their hearts. Socrates initiated Western philosophy and the development of free speech. Confucius created his ideology that was deeply rooted in his contemporary Chinese society, and this deeply influenced the state institutions. His thoughts became adopted as the central tenet for the suffering Chinese nation after so many misfortunes over more than two thousand years and still continue to this day.

Confucius, who was born in BC 551 in Qufu county, Shangdong province, China during the Spring and Autumn period, was an ancient Chinese philosopher, an educationalist, and the creator of the Confucian ideology. With a strong social responsibility and a sense of mission, he emphasised self-cultivation, family-regulation, state-governance, and the promotion of peace. He advocated 'benevolence, justice, ritual, wisdom, belief, harmony and the golden mean'.

'Benevolence' is to love people and is humane and full of compassion. 'Justice' is used to uphold righteousness and maintain integrity. 'Ritual' is to pay attention to propriety and give respect to others. 'Wisdom' is to enhance quality and to serve society. 'Belief' is to be credible and lawful, keeping one's word. After Confucius died, his disciples and their successors recorded his words, deeds, and thoughts, and compiled them into a classic called *The Analects* that is used like a type of Chinese bible.

Confucian ideology has deeply influenced the Chinese social fabric through its adoption and promotion for more than two thousand years. It has also played a positive role in the development of cultural philosophies and religious systems in the East Asian region and other countries as it spread all over the world. The Confucius Institutes that we see today are all named after him.

For example, after Confucian ideology had spread through the Korean Peninsula, it gradually became the orthodoxy of the feudal dynasties. Today in Japan it has integrated into the nation's thinking and lifestyle, behaviour, and philosophy. In South Korea there are not only the Confucian associations and research institutes, but it is also studied as a specialised subject that has been set up in more than twenty universities. In Vietnam it has also influenced the development of various initiatives.

The original French version of *An Introduction to The Analects of Confucius*, that was published in 1688, was presented to Chinese President Xi Jinping as a gift from the nation by his French counterpart, Emmanuel Macron, when the two leaders met in Nice, France on 24 March 2019. The early translation of *The Analects* of Confucius inspired French thinkers Montesquieu and Voltaire, said Macron. Voltaire once said: "that saint is Confucius, He sees himself as tall and is the lawmaker of mankind."

Some Western countries may have ideological views about Confucius. The reason is that during the Han dynasty, the rulers paid the supreme tribute to Confucianism whilst rejecting all other schools of thought. The orthodox Confucianism served as the state ideology and helped to establish its foundation in Chinese feudal dynasties for more than two thousand years. What it advocates is 'the divine right of the king', 'the Three Cardinal Guides and Five Constant Virtues', 'be loyal to the king', etc. that have become a tool for the ruler to manipulate people's thoughts.

In fact, the philosophy of Confucius has gradually spread overseas, advocating the 'Golden Mean' with its moral power. What it now embodies is the precept that 'peace and harmony should prevail' and 'building a community with a shared future for humanity'. This provides a positive solution and idea to address the growing international struggles in society. This shows that Confucian ideology paradoxically is not only behind the times but also will continue to affect Chinese civilization and even play a positive role in world culture.

Chinese civilization is extensive and profound. When Confucius was alive, in ancient times, they usually used a classical style of writing that was concise and obscure. The aim of our book is to make it easier for Westerners to better understand Chinese stories. We have selected some stories about Confucius and his disciples that are full of wisdom and are inspirational. They guide us to best deal with others, better do things, know the world, and make it better.

Note:三纲五常：

The Three Cardinal Guides (ruler guides subject, father guides son and husband guides wife) and Five Constant Virtues {benevolence, righteousness, propriety, knowledge, and belief} -- principle of feudal moral conduct."

孔子简介

古印度佛陀、中国孔子和希腊苏格拉底,都是人类的古圣先贤。佛陀使全世界信徒的痛苦得到解脱,救赎了他们的心灵。苏格拉底开启了西方哲学和言论自由的探索。孔子创造的哲学思想扎根于中国社会,并深刻影响了国家制度。他的思想成为苦难的中华民族两千多年历经劫难却生生不息的文明核心,并延续至今,历久弥新。

公元前551年,孔子出生于鲁国陬邑(今山东曲阜),是中国古代思想家、教育家,儒家学派创始人。孔子开创的儒家学派,有着强烈的社会责任感和使命感。强调"修身、齐家、治国、平天下"。倡导"仁义礼智信"、"和谐"、"中庸之道"。"仁",仁就是"爱人",就是以人为本,富有爱心。"义",就是坚持正义,保持节操。"礼",就是注重礼仪,尊重他人。"智",就是提高素质,服务社会。"信",就是诚信守法,一诺千金。孔子修订了《诗》《书》《礼》《乐》《易》《春秋》六经。他去世后,其弟子及其再传弟子把孔子及其弟子的言行语录和思想记录下来，整理编成儒家经典《论语》，它所记述的孔子言录，可以说是我们中国人的"圣经"。

经过两千多年的传承和发展，儒家学说对中国社会产生了深远的影响，并且传播至世界各地，对东亚地区和其他国家的文化思想和宗教体系的发展产生了积极作用。今天我们所看到的孔子学院，就是以他来命名的。

儒家思想传入朝鲜半岛后，逐渐成为朝鲜封建社会的正统思想。而在日本，如今儒家思想已经融入日本民族的思维方式、生活方式、行为方式和哲学中。韩国不仅拥有儒教学会、儒教文化研究所等机构，而且在20多所大学里还设有专门研究儒家思想的学科。儒家还影响着越南的各项事业发展。

2019年3月24日，中国主席习近平在法国尼斯会见法国总统马克龙。马克龙向习近平赠送1688年法国出版的首部《论语导读》法文版原著。马克龙说，《论语》的早期导读和翻译曾对孟德斯鸠和伏尔泰的哲学思想给予启发。伏尔泰视孔子为真正的哲学家，他曾说"那个圣人，孔夫子，认为自己受命于天，为人类建立道德法则。"

西方有些国家可能对孔子存在着意识形态的看法，原因是自汉朝"罢黜百家、独尊儒术"以来，中国两千多年以来都利用儒学作为统治阶级服务的思想，其提倡的"君权神授"、"三纲五常"、"忠君"等思想通常成为被统治阶级利成为钳制人民思想的工具。

而事实上，以孔子为代表的儒家文化，不靠武力，不靠手段，却能远播海外，以无形的道德力量渗透着和谐中庸的理念，体现在现在就是协和万邦、人类命运共同体等倡议，为现实社会愈演愈烈的国际斗争提出了积极的解决办法和理念。这说明，孔子的思想没有过时，而且将继续影响着中华文明，甚至对世界文化产生积极作用。

中华文明博大精深，孔子所在的中国古代，通常用文言文来撰写书籍，而且言简意赅，有些甚至晦涩难懂。本书的目的是为了便于外国朋友更能了解中国故事而编撰的普及读本，所以选取了一些孔子以及弟子的小故事，它们通常寓意丰富、发人深省。这些故事启迪着我们应该怎样做人、做事、应该怎样去认识世界、改造世界。

Stories about Confucius' Eagerness to Learn.

IN CONFUCIAN WORKS, LEARNING IS mentioned many times. *The Analects* initial mention of learning begins in the first chapter. Confucius wasn't born with knowledge. There wasn't such a man in the world before and there won't be in the future. His talents and capabilities derived from his learning and diligence. There are several stories that can truly reflect Confucius' rigorous style of study.

孔子好学的故事

在孔子的著述中,多次提到学习,论语的开篇就是《学而》。孔子并不是生而知之,世界上从前没有,将来也不会有这种生而知之的人,他的才干和能力都是来自于他的好学与勤奋。以下几个故事能够真实的反应孔子好学严谨的治学风貌。

Chapter One

The Meeting between
Confucius and Lao Zi

CONFUCIUS AND LAO ZI ARE two of the most famous sages within the ancient Chinese tradition, representing, respectively, the Confucian (named after Confucius) and Daoist philosophies. Both lived during the same historical period. Lao Zi was born in BC 571 and Confucius, some twenty years later, in BC 551. Generally speaking, people from different academic and philosophical backgrounds at that time were often at odds, but this was not the case with these two. Confucius visited his contemporary Lao Zi several times, the latter having no reservations in teaching all that he knew to the younger man.

In the year BC 518, when Confucius was 33 years of age, he made a special visit to consult Lao Zi about the Rite of the Zhou dynasty. Lao Zi was the official historian of the Zhou dynasty (a position similar to that of a curator of a national museum and library today). He received Confucius and showed him the whole range of classics and cultural relics that had been collected during the Zhou dynasty. He guided him around the temple and to the places where the king worshipped Heaven and Earth. Lao Zi imparted what he knew to Confucius.

Upon their parting, Lao Zi said to Confucius: 'You made reference to "the Rite" and of the people who initiated these, that their bones have already rotted. Only views still exist. The man who is good at business often hides his goods. The noble gentleman always looks humble and stupid. I heard that a gentleman should take advantage of any opportunity. If no opportunities arise, then no matter how capable you are, your skills cannot be applied. You should be humble and rid yourself of any ambition to seek achievements. All of your desires for fame and fortune are of no benefit to the body and mind.'

Lao Zi's avoidance of formal academic groups and his broad mind deeply influenced Confucius. When he returned to the Lu state, he said to his disciples: 'With regard to a bird, I know that it can fly. Fish can swim. A beast can run. Catching a beast using a net, fishing with a line, felling a bird with a bow, but how to tackle a dragon? Currently, I believe that Lao Zi is most probably like a dragon. Only a dragon can be described as impossible to know. It flies in the clouds and is unpredictable".

Confucius further remarked: 'When a man has acquired wisdom in the morning, he may be content to die in the evening.'

It can be seen that Confucius had a great thirst for knowledge. He learned from Lao Zi and broke the barriers between the different academic opinions that were abroad at that time. Lao Zi's unreserved teaching also reflects his self-cultivation and the broad mindset of an ancient Chinese scholar. It is precisely because the ancient Chinese academic groups were able to absorb and develop mutually from the Confucians and Daoist sources that traditional Chinese culture was able to fuse organically. This is the foundation for the precious spiritual wealth of the Chinese nation that has continued for thousands of years, and the longer it lasts, the better it endures. This is what the Chinese scholars have inherited today.

Note:周礼:

The Rite of the Zhou dynasty was the name given to the political protocols and legal system of the time. The Rituals of the Zhou dynasty consisted of five parts. Sacrifices were an auspicious ritual. Funerals were an ominous ritual. Army service was a military ritual. Hospitality was a guest ritual. Marriages were a wedding ritual.

孔子和老子的会面

孔子和老子是中国传统文化中两位标志性的人物，他们分别代表着儒家和道家，他们的学说对于中华民族的文化都起着十分重要的作用。有趣的是，他们两位都出生在同一时期，老子出生在约公元前571年，孔子出生在公元前551年，一般而言，有着不同学术派别和学术观点的人往往有很多对立的地方，但孔子和老子却不是这样，孔子不远万里，曾几次去拜访老子，而老子都毫无保留、全部奉告，留下了一段佳话。

公元前518年，孔子三十三岁时，他曾专程向老子请教周礼。当时老子是周朝的守藏室之史（类似于现在文物、博物、图书馆馆长）。老子接待了孔子并让他参阅了周朝所藏的丰富的典籍、文物，还带他参观了名堂、太庙和天子郊祭天、社祭地的场所，让孔子学会了更多传统知识，丰富了学术内容。"临分手时，老子还告诫孔子说："你所说的礼，倡导它的人和骨头都已经腐烂了，只有他的言论还在。况且君子时运来了就驾着车出去做官，生不逢时，就像蓬草一样随风飘转。我听说，善于经商的人把货物隐藏起来，好像什么东西也没有，君子具有高尚的的品德，他的容貌谦虚得像愚钝的人。君子应乘势而起；时运未到，任你本领再大，仍不为世所用。你应少一些骄狂之气，去除渴望建功立业的欲望之心，所有功名利禄之念都是无益于身心的。"老子这种不计门庭的胸怀，洒脱的胸襟和广博的知识，再一次得到了孔子的敬重。孔子回到鲁国后，对弟子说："鸟，我知道它能飞；鱼，我知道它能游；兽，我知道它能跑。会跑的可以织网捕获它，会游的可制成丝线去钓它，会飞的可以用箭去射它。至于龙，我就不知道该怎么办了，它是驾着风而飞腾升天的。我今天见到的老子，大概就是龙吧！老子就像龙一样，乘云而上，高深莫测。

孔子还说："朝闻道，夕死可矣。"意思是早晨学到了知识，那么即便当晚死去，也没有什么遗憾了。

从他们之间的交往，我们可以看出孔子求知若渴的学习态度和老子广博的胸怀。正是由于以儒家和道家为代表的中国古代学派能够包容并蓄，使得中华优秀传统文明有机融合，成为几千年来绵延不绝，愈久弥新的宝贵精神财富，这也是今天中国的学者谦虚好学的涵养和胸怀的文化来源。

注：周礼：即周朝的政治文化和法律制度。西周五礼：是汉族礼仪总称。以祭祀之事为吉礼，丧葬之事为凶礼，军旅之事为军礼，宾客之事为宾礼，冠婚之事为嘉礼，合称五礼。即吉礼、凶礼、军礼、宾礼、嘉礼。

Chapter Two

Confucius Learned from a Seven-Year-Old Child

CONFUCIUS SAID: 'THE YOUNGER GENERATION will surpass the current one – how does anyone know that the future will be inferior to the present day?' From this, we can see that Confucius was very sure about what the future generations would achieve. He was not ashamed to consult people who were in a lower social position to himself. He even learned from a seven-year-old child named Xiang Tuo.

As Confucius was travelling around, he saw three children. Two of them were playing but the other was just standing on his own. Confucius was curious about this, so he asked the child why he didn't play with the other two children.

The boy answered in a serious tone: 'Rough behaviour can hurt one, pushing and pulling can also do similarly; to say the least, it does no good to tear one's clothes, so I don't want to play with them. Why is this curious?'

A moment later, the child built a castle with muddy soil and sat inside it. He just stayed there and didn't want to get out of the way for Confucius who, therefore, enquired: 'Why don't you make way for my cart?' The child answered: 'I have heard that a cart should go around a castle but never that a castle should give way to a cart.'

Confucius was stunned, and he thought that the child was very articulate and that this was incredible. He praised him and said: 'You know a lot for such a young age!' The child said: 'I heard that within three days fish can swim, rabbits can run, and horses can walk alongside the mare. These are natural things, no matter whether old or young.' Confucius sighed and said: 'Well, now I know that young people are marvellous!'

As a sage, Confucius learned from the child. This attitude was praiseworthy then and still is today. It tells us that Confucius was extremely open-minded, practical, and realistic. His open attitude to learning, spirit of seeking truth from facts, and boldness of vision are all positive traits that we should follow today. There is no end to learning, even if one day you reach the peak of knowledge. You should still keep an open mind and learn from people of all ages and vocations.

孔子向孩童学习

孔子说:"年轻人可敬畏啊,怎么就知道未来的人就不如当今的人呢?"孔子非常肯定后来者可能取得的成就,他不耻下问,甚至拜只有七岁的项橐为师。

孔子在游历的时候,碰见三个小孩,有两个正在玩耍,另一个小孩却站在旁边。孔子觉得奇怪,就问站着的小孩为什么不和大家一起玩。

小孩很认真地回答:"激烈的打闹能害人的性命,拉拉扯扯的玩耍也会伤人的身体;再退一步说,撕破了衣服,也没有什么好处。所以我不愿和他们玩。这有什么可奇怪的呢?"

过了一会,小孩用泥土堆成一座城堡,自己坐在里面,好久不出来,也不给准备动身的孔子让路。孔子忍不住又问:"你坐在里面,为什么不避让车子?""我只听说车子要绕城走,没有听说过城堡还要避车子的!"孩子说。

孔子非常惊讶,觉得这么小的孩子,竟如此会说话,实在是了不起,于是赞叹他说:"你这么小的年纪,懂得的事理真不少呀!"小孩却回答说:"我听人说,鱼生下来,三天就会游泳，兔生下来，三天就能在地里跑，马生下来，三天就可跟着母马行走。这些都是自然的事，有什么大小可言呢？"孔子不由感叹他说："好啊，我现在才知道少年人实在了不起呀！"

孔子以圣人之身，不耻拜孩童为师，其举天下称道，所以流传至今。这个故事告诉我们，就算是被称之为万圣师表的孔子都会虚心向孩童学习，他虚怀若谷的学习态度，实事求是的求学精神，海纳百川的胸怀气魄，都是我们学习的榜样。学无止境，即便有一天你登上了知识的巅峰，仍然要一个空杯的心态，向各行各业、各个年龄阶段的人学习。

Chapter Three

Confucius Learned from His Disciples

CONFUCIUS SAID: 'WHEN THREE MEN meet together, the one who is anxious to study can always learn something from the other two. He can profit by the good example of the one and avoid that of the bad.'

Confucius was adept at teaching his disciples to adopt a broad approach to learning. He thought that not only should disciples learn from the teachers but that this learning of their strengths should also apply vice versa. Observing their weaknesses, we should check ourselves to see if we also have any, then we should correct them. This can be seen from the dialogues between Confucius and his disciples as follows.

One day, Confucius went on a trip with the disciple Zixia who wanted to know his teacher's evaluation of other disciples, so he asked: 'Sir, what do you think of Yan Hui?'

Confucius answered: 'He is benevolent and righteous and can be a comfort in poverty.'

Zixia asked again: 'How about Zigong?'

Confucius answered: 'He is more eloquent than me.'

Zixia continued: 'How about Zilu?'

Confucius said: 'He is chivalrous and brave. He is the bravest among us.'

Zixia continued: 'How about Zizhang?'

Confucius said: 'Zizhang is calm when something crops up. He is sober-minded and solemn, so he has a stricter style than me.'

From the dialogue we discover that Confucius believed that everybody has their own strengths and that we should recognise and overcome our shortcomings. He also said: 'To understand what it is that you know and what is unknown, this is real wisdom.'

One time, disciple Fan Chi asked Confucius about growing crops and vegetables. Confucius answered: 'I am inferior to a farmer or a vegetable grower.' A scholar is certainly not as experienced as a farmer. Confucius couldn't claim to know everything in the world. In the face of disciples' questions, he was honest enough to admit that he was not as good as a farmer. This is the correct attitude that a true scholar should have.

Seeking truth from facts and being open-minded is the attitude that a scholar should have. Pretending to know what you actually don't understand or presuming on your seniority can obstruct academic progress. Do not fix on the old knowledge but, with an open heart, embrace the new. Do not place limits on your existing identifications but have the courage to learn from people of all vocations and ages. This reflects Chinese traditional culture – that of seeking harmony but not uniformity and finding common ground whilst setting aside differences. This was advocated by Chinese ancient sages represented by Confucius and is broad and full of life.

孔子向弟子学习

孔子说"三人行必有我师。择其善者而从之,其不善者而改之。"孔子采用循循善诱的方式教育弟子要虚心学习,不仅是弟子向老师学习,孔子同时也向他的弟子学习。学习他们的优点和长处。至于别人的缺点,则要对照自己检查有没有,加以改正。这点可以从他和弟子子夏的对话中看出来:

有一天,孔子偕子夏出游,子夏想了解他对其他弟子的评价。他问孔子:"颜回为人怎么样?"

孔子沉吟了一下答道:"颜回喜好仁义,乐善好施,安于贫困。"

子夏又问:"那子贡呢?"。

孔子说:"他口若悬河、善于雄辩,他的口才比我强。"

子夏接着问"那子路呢?"

孔子说:"子路行侠仗义、勇猛无比。要说勇武精神,我们都不如他。"

子夏又说"那子张呢?"

孔子说:"子张遇事冷静、不苟言笑,为人处世庄重严谨,这些方面比我要强。"

从孔子和子夏的对话看出，孔子认为每个人都有值得学习的地方，要取人之长，补己之短。孔子还说："知之为知之，不知为不知，是知也。"（懂得了就是懂得了，不懂就是没有懂，这才是真正的智慧呀！）

有一次，孔子的学生樊迟，曾向老师问种庄稼和蔬菜的道理，孔子都回答："我不如老农民"、"我不如老菜农"。学者在种地这方面肯定不如有实践经验的农民，孔子也不可能什么都知道，面对学生的提问，他勇于承认自己不如一个老菜农。这才是学者应有的态度。

实事求是、虚心向学是一个学者应有的态度。不懂装懂、倚老卖老会阻碍学术的进步。不僵化于旧知，敞开心怀迎接新知，不拘泥于已有的身份，而是勇于向各行各业，各个年龄的人求教。这体现了以孔子为代表的古代圣贤所倡导的和而不同、求同存异的中国传统文化兼收并蓄的包容性和生命力。

Chapter Four

The True Meaning of Learning

AT THE AGE OF 15, CONFUCIUS made up his mind to give himself up to serious studies. He worked hard and by the time that he reached 30 years of age, he had formed his opinions and judgments and so he was able to establish himself in society by relying on his accumulated knowledge. By the age of 40, he had developed a level of cultivation such that he could avoid outside temptation. At 50, he had cultivated a calm mind such that he could peacefully face his destiny. At 60, he could correctly absorb all kinds of criticism and distinguish between true and false. At 70, he achieved a superior level of knowledge and cultivation. He could follow whatever his heart desired without transgressing any rules and laws.

Water has its source whilst trees have their roots. The reason Confucius become an exemplar in China and throughout the world certainly had much to do with his early years. This really has a lot to do with the teaching of his mother, who was an ordinary but great woman.

Confucius' mother, Yan Zhengzai, married his father, a warrior who was already 60 years of age, when she was in her early twenties. Unfortunately, his father died when Confucius was only 3 years of age and Yan Zhengzai looked after him alone from then on. They moved to Qufu, the capital of the Lu state. During the Spring and Autumn period China was in chaos, and rituals went out of fashion. People in the warring countries thought that the institutions and relics of the Zhou dynasty were alive in the Lu state. There was even a saying that the rituals of the Zhou dynasty were all in the Lu state. Growing up in such a cultural environment, Confucius was able to profit from studying in such conditions.

His mother did any type of hard work that was required in order to make a living. She toiled tirelessly to support her son, who was her hope and love, for his livelihood and education. It was her diligence, courage and love of education that made Confucius become a man who was an embodiment of Heaven and Earth and who was determined to serve his country and society.

Those who just know how to learn are not as good as those who love to do so. Those who love to learn are inferior to those who find their joy in it. Confucius once said that his talents weren't different to ordinary people. The knowledge and moral achievements he acquired were because of his eagerness to learn. There are many people who excel in learning. Even many treacherous ministers in China from all dynasties were knowledgeable, but they didn't have the right attitude to life and ethics. They just acquired superficial knowledge but didn't know how to be good people, resulting in chaos in the state so that their names lived on in infamy. Only by setting high aspirations and broad ambitions, and not being driven by social desires but persevering in the pursuit of truth, can our knowledge and actions be as one. Then we can utilise our learning and benefit society.

学习的真谛

孔子说：吾十有五而志于学，三十而立，四十而不惑，五十而知天命，六十而耳顺，七十而从心所欲不逾矩。孔子十五岁的时候便立志于学，他勤奋学习，到了三十岁才说自己可以凭借学识立足于社会了，到了四十岁有了一定的修养基础，才可以避免外界的诱惑了，五十岁他有了一种淡然的心境，可以从容面对那些不受人力控制的"天命"，到了六十岁，他能正确对待各种言论，分辨真假是非，七十岁时他的见闻、学识、修养都炉火纯青，此时不用刻意，随心的言行也不会逾越道德规矩了。

水有源，树有根，孔子之所以能成为对中国乃至世界都有深刻影响的伟大人物，当然与他的少年时代有很大的关系。这一基础与他平凡而又伟大的母亲对他的教导紧密相关。

孔子的母亲颜征在不到 20 岁的时候嫁给了孔子的父亲，一位 60 多岁的勇士。可孔子不到三岁时，父亲就突然去世了。才 20 出头的颜征在带着三岁的孔子离开孔家，搬到了鲁国都城曲阜。春秋末年礼崩乐坏，历经战乱的诸国当中，人们普遍认为周朝的典章文物都在鲁国，以及周礼尽在鲁国的说法。孔子的母亲让孩子在这样的环境中成长，更能提供有利的学习条件耳濡目染的受到熏陶。

母亲坚持做各种杂役粗活来维持生计，她对儿子的生活和教育付出超出常人的辛劳，儿子是母亲全部的希望和心头的爱。正是母亲的勤劳、勇敢和对孩子爱的教育使孔子成为了一个怀天地之心，报效祖国报效社会的人。

孔子常说，"知之者不如好之者，好之者不如乐之者。"知道学习的人比不上爱好学习的人，爱好学习的人比不上以学习为快乐的人。孔子曾谦逊的说自己的资质和普通人并没有什么太大的区别，所获得的知识和道德成就都是因为好学而得到的。世上会做学问的人很多，中国历朝历代就出了很多很有学问的奸臣，可他们没有正确的人生观，价值观。只学习了表面的文章，却没有做好人生的文章，致使祸国殃民、遗臭万年。只有树立了崇高的志向，拥有远大的抱负，不被世俗欲望所驱使，锲而不舍的追求真理，才能知行合一、学以致用、造福社会。

Chapter Five

Versatile Confucius

CONFUCIUS WAS BORN INTO POVERTY but grew up to master a wide range of skills. He excelled in rituals, music, archery, as a coachman, (the horse-drawn buggy was the most important method of transportation in ancient China, so this type of skill was essential), calligraphy and mathematics. He was a truly versatile man.

The Analects recorded that Confucius' appreciation of ancient music had reached the level of an obsession. When in the Qi state, he heard the musical score named 'Shao Yue' and became immersed in it. He gave himself up to the study of it for three months, even to the sacrifice of his daily meals. He said: 'I would never have thought that music could be brought to such perfection.' It was Confucius' eagerness to learn and apply effort that led to him becoming so obsessed that he even ignored the taste of meat. This is the origin of a Chinese idiom: 'Three months ignoring the taste of meat.'

There is also a story of Confucius learning to play a guqin (a traditional instrument invented in China) from Shi Xiangzi who was also a classical scholar. Shi Xiangzi may never have seen anyone in his whole life like Confucius, who learned the guqin and whose skills were already excellent but still unsatisfactory to him. After hearing

Shi Xiangzi's playing, Confucius made up his mind to learn more and raise his skill to a new level. Two weeks later, he continued to play the same melody. Even Shi Xiangzi thought his standard was quite good so advised him to learn a new one. Confucius said: 'I've already acquainted myself with the form of the music but still haven't grasped the method.'

Several days later, Confucius had already acquired the skill, but he said: 'I haven't mastered the artistic side yet'. Another few days later, the teacher said: 'You have already grasped the artistic aspect and can now learn a new piece of music.' Confucius said: 'I haven't understood the writer yet.'

Finally, one day, Confucius stood up with the melody lingering in the air, opened the window and looked into the distant sky and said: 'I now know who he is. He is tall and of a dark complexion. His eyes are bright and eager, and he looks like a king. If not Emperor Zhou Wen, then who else could write such a melody?' After hearing this, Shi Xiangzi quickly stood up and twice bowed to Confucius and said: 'That's what my teacher told me when I was learning from him. The name of the musician is Wen Wangcao!'

Not only having excelled in playing the guqin, *The Liji* recorded that Confucius was also adept at shooting. One day, an archery event was held in the county. There were many spectators who were gathered around to watch Confucius' performance. If not to see a superior skill, there would not have been so many people in attendance. It was legendary that Confucius' mastery of the horse-drawn buggy was even better than his skill at archery. *Huai Nanzi* recorded that Confucius was skilled in running and even described how he could keep up with an onrushing rabbit.

When teaching his disciples, Confucius once said: 'A gentleman should be versatile, know both the past and the present, speak appropriately and behave generously.' He hoped that his disciples would not only attain superior skills but also develop in an all-round way. The mission of a gentleman is to bring peace and stability to the state. He can successfully undertake diplomacy, hold the world in his heart and be beneficial to all things. He emphasised that learning should be appropriate and practicable. Confucius was such a person who loved to learn, excelled in it, and regarded it as a pleasure. He was such a brilliant man of wide knowledge.

Note: During the periods of the Spring and Autumn and the Warring State, ritual, musical, archery, driving, calligraphy and mathematics were six skills that it was considered that a scholar should learn. Archery and driving the horse-drawn buggy were military skills because there were many wars at that time, so those two were very important. Rituals and music were favoured by the institution. Calligraphy and mathematics were necessary skills.

多才多艺的孔子

孔子年少时出身贫苦，所以他在年轻的时候就掌握了很多谋生的技能，他精通礼法、乐舞、射箭、驾车、书法和算数，是个多才多艺的人。

《论语.述而》记载孔子欣赏古乐已经到了痴迷的程度。他在齐国听到美妙绝伦的《韶乐》，沉浸其中，三个月都尝不出肉的味道来，他感叹道："想不到韶乐的美竟然达到了这样的地步！正是孔子的好学与投入，学习起来到了入迷的程度，连吃肉都不知道味道了。这就是成语三月不知肉味的来历。

孔子向师襄子学琴故事也非常经典。师襄子也许一生也没有见到过能够如孔子这样学琴的人。本来孔子的琴艺已经相当好了，但他不满足。在他听到师襄子的弹奏后，就下定决心要向师襄子学习，好让自己的琴技提高到新的境界。已经弹奏了半个多月了，孔子还在继续学习同一支曲子。连师襄子都觉得已经相当好了，就劝他："这个曲子你确实已经会了，学首新的吧。"孔子却说："曲调是会了，可奏曲的技巧尚未学好。"

过了几日，师襄子听着觉得连技艺也熟了，又劝他："技艺已经学好了，该学新的曲子了。"孔子还沉浸在曲调中，过了好一会才回答说："我还没能领会这首曲子的志趣神韵呢。"又过了一些日子，细心的师襄子察觉出自己的学生已经掌握了曲子的志趣和神韵，便再次郑重的劝到："志趣神韵都有了，可以学新的曲子了"。但想不到孔子坚持要继续学习同一支曲子。他向师襄子请求："再等等吧，等我体察出这个作者是谁并想象出他的精神风貌，再学新的曲子吧。"

终于有一天，孔子在琴声缭绕的余音中站起来，推开窗子，向着遥远的天边抬头仰望，许久才若有所思的说："我知道他是谁了：那人皮肤深黑，体形颀长，眼光明亮远大，像个统治四方诸侯的王者，若不是周文王还有谁能作这首乐曲呢?"师襄子听到后，赶紧起身拜了两拜，回答道："老琴师传授此曲时就是这样说的,这支曲子叫做《文王操》啊！。

不只是弹琴的技艺高超，《礼记》中记载，孔子还擅长"射艺"。有一天举行"乡射"，观者如堵墙，如果不是一流的技术，也不会吸引这么多人来看。据说孔子的驾车本领比射箭还厉害，《淮南子》还称孔子很擅长跑步，形容他"足蹑郊(狡)兔"意思是连奔跑的兔子都能追到。

孔子教育他的弟子时曾说："君子不器"，"志于道，据于德，依于仁，游于艺。"他认为君子应该多才多艺，博览古今，言辞得体，举止大方。他希望他的弟子不仅具备高尚的品德，还应有娴熟精湛的技艺，要均衡全面发展。君子的使命是在内可以定国安邦。在外可以不辱使命，心怀天下，泽被万方。他强调学以致用，学习用于实践，孔子就是这样一个爱学习，善学习，以学习为乐，广泛涉猎，博学多才的人。

注释：礼乐射御书数为春秋战国时期读书人必须学习的六种技艺，分别为学习礼法、乐舞、射箭、驾车、书法和算术。其中射箭、驾车（御战车、驾车）为军事技能。射御主要是指个人战斗技能，因为过去国家间纷争非常多，经常有战争发生，所以射御在当时是非常重要的，礼和乐偏重于制度，书法和算数是必备技能。

Confucius' Benevolence

THE ANALECTS MENTIONS THE WORD 'benevolence' 109 times, explaining it from different perspectives. Benevolence is the core of Confucianism adopting it as its lofty tenet. Confucius' benevolent ideology embodies personal moral cultivation, filial piety, a sense of benevolence, and other moral rules and practical action. Benevolence is the ideal quality for a Confucian and has been adopted as the spiritual guidance of the Chinese people who take filial piety as a key principle. It also had a great influence on later generations.

孔子的"仁"

一部《论语》,居然有109次提到仁,并且从各种角度对仁进行阐述。仁,是儒学的核心思想,也是一个很高的境界。孔子的仁爱思想体现在个人的道德修养、孝敬父母、义利关系等等行为道德规范和实际行动中。仁是儒家理想的人格目标,也成为中华民族仁孝为本的精神财富,对后世产生了极大的影响。

Chapter Six

What is 'benevolence'?

MANY DISCIPLES ASKED CONFUCIUS THE question, 'What on earth is "benevolence"?"' Perhaps it was because students were taught according to their natural ability that Confucius replied to each differently, in order to optimise his teaching and act in accord with their make-up.

First of all, disciple Yan Yuan asked about benevolence. Confucius answered: 'Restraining desires and controlling words and deeds, this is benevolence.' This is the core principle used here for Confucius' explanation of benevolence and is the central content of *The Analects*. Confucius pointed out that to be benevolent, you need to restrain desires and control words and actions, so ritual is based on benevolence whilst the former is the approach to the latter. Benevolence emphasises the inner heart; ritual places the emphasis on deeds.

Disciple Fan Chi three times asked about benevolence. On the most famous occasion, Confucius answered: 'To love people." Fan Chi again asked about wisdom. Confucius answered : 'To know people.' Confucius told Fan Chi to care for people and treat others equally and respect them, this is a great love. Confucius' advice to love people wasn't abstract but was made on the basis of 'wisdom'. His proposal was to understand others, distinguish between true and false, promote righteous people whilst avoiding the deceitful. Benevolence and wisdom are closely related, therefore, he said, 'Only the benevolent can love and hate people. The benevolent can treat people impartially and so he is the only one that can do so correctly.'

Disciple Zhong Gong asked about benevolence. Confucius said: 'Be sure to treat all people equally, respecting everyone, whether kings or ordinary people, you should be polite as if all of them were distinguished guests. Undertaking labour should be as serious as attaching importance to great sacrifices. Do not impose on others that which you yourself do not want to do, put yourself in the place of another, pay attention to morality and do not attach to self-interest. Then we will receive no complaints and will not be resented by others.'

Zi Gong asked: 'If there is someone who can benefit people and help everyone to live a good life, can it be considered to be benevolence?' Confucius answered: 'This is more than benevolence: it is a sagacity. Even Rao and Shun [Chinese ancient sages] find it hard to do so.'

What Zi Gong talks about not only presupposes a very high level of moral cultivation but also achievement of a profound political appreciation that the ordinary people couldn't achieve. Confucius thus stated: 'They are willing to stand up, they want to reach. It can be said be the sign of benevolence.' To hope to achieve something but also to make others achieve as well. Treating others, the way you want to be treated this is the way to achieve benevolence.'

Actually, there are still many examples of Confucius' disciples asking about benevolence in *The Analects*. Confucius said benevolent governance is just like the Plough – although standing there motionless, other stars will unceasingly surround it. Confucius' benevolence is equally like a star shining with the light of wisdom, witnessing the great changes spanning time and space from the ancient to the present, converging into a sea with the light of humanity from the East and West.

什么是"仁"

孔子有很多弟子都问过他，到底什么是"仁"，但他按照因材施教的方式会根据每个弟子的特性进行有针对性的回复，实行教化。

首先是弟子颜渊问仁。孔子回答："克己复礼为仁。"克己复礼是孔子关于什么是仁的主要解释，也是整部论语最核心的内容。孔子指出，要想达到仁，就应该克制自己的私欲，用礼来节制自己的言行。所以，礼以仁为基础，仁以礼为途径；仁重于内心，礼重于外行。

弟子樊迟曾三次问仁。最为经典的是这一次孔子的回答："爱人"。樊迟又问什么是智，孔子回答："知人。"孔子是告诉樊迟要有爱心，要把他人当作平等的人来对待，尊重他人，这是一种大爱。但儒家所说的爱人不是毫无分别的爱，而是要在"智"的基础上，了解他人，能够分辩是非，选拔正义的人，远离奸佞的人。所以仁和智是息息相关的。所以他说："唯仁者能爱人，能恶人。"只有仁者才能公正无私地去喜爱人、憎恶人。

弟子仲弓问仁时，孔子告诉仲弓：一定要平等待人，出了门，对任何人都要有礼貌、尊重，不管是国君还是老百姓，都要如看待贵宾一样。役使百姓，要像重视大的祭祀一样严肃认真。自己不愿意的事，就不要强加给别人。推己及人，重视道义、不坏私利，最后才能达到不怨天尤人，也不招致别人的怨尤。（子曰："出门如见大宾，使民如承大祭；己所不欲，勿施于人。在邦无怨，在家无怨"。）

子贡问："如果有这么一个人，能广泛地给人民以好处，又能帮助大家都生活得好，可以算得上是仁了吗？"孔子回答："这岂止是仁，简直是圣了！尧舜都难以做到！"子贡提出的博施惠利于百姓而能济大众的行为不仅需要有极高的道德修养，而且还要有较高的政治地位，不是一般人可以做到的。所以孔子说"夫仁者，己欲立而立人，己欲达而达人。能近取譬，可谓仁之方也。"能够做到希望自己有所成就，也要让别人有所成就，自己要显达，也要帮助别人一同显达。凡事能推己及人，这可以说就是实现仁的方法了。

其实《论语》中，学生们这样问仁于老师的例子还有很多，孔子说仁政就如同北斗星一样，虽然站在那里不动，而其他很多星星也会心悦诚服的环绕着它。孔子的仁道情怀，就如同这闪耀着智慧之光的星辰，见证着古往今来跨越时空的巨变，汇聚成东方和西方人性光芒的海洋。

Chapter Seven

The Benevolence Pioneer

CONFUCIUS NOT ONLY TAUGHT HIS disciples in words but also set an example with practical actions.

Once, when passing by Mount Tai, Confucius saw a woman weeping in front of a tomb. He let Zilu ask the woman why she was crying. She answered: 'My father-in-law was attacked and killed by a tiger, then my husband, and now my son' Confucius asked: 'Why don't you just leave here?' She answered: 'Because there are no cruel decrees here.' Confucius said: 'You should remember that tyranny is more ferocious than a tiger.'

The story reflects Confucius' opposition to tyranny and his promotion of benevolent governance. He advocated reflecting upon the situation of people and cherishing their strengths. He was opposed to arbitrarily killing and preying on people.

Although Confucius was not in a high position, he could sympathise with people's sufferings, thus reflecting his great compassion. There is a short story that also reflects Confucius' advocacy of putting people first.

Once, after his return from the royal court, Confucius' stable was found to be on fire, so he asked: 'Did anyone get hurt?' He didn't ask about the horses but rather of the people. This reflected his benevolence. Confucius lived in the period of the Spring and Autumn and the Warning State, during which time a horse was accorded a higher status and was more precious than a servant or a horseman. Confucius asked about the people first and then the horses, reflecting the consistent thought of 'the benevolent loves others and cares for them'.

Confucius' affection for people also reflects his love of life. Human sacrifices were often advocated in ancient times. With the evolution of society, there was a reduction of such inhumanity, and it was gradually substituted with animal sacrifices. Instead, pottery figures were buried with the dead by the time of Spring and Autumn period, when Confucius lived. Even in this way, Confucius was disgusted. It was recorded in 'Mencius' writings that Confucius resentfully asked: 'Who started this first?'

In Confucius' philosophy, benevolence is the highest moral standard, and this should be one's lifetime's aim. During chaotic times, the relationship between states and peoples deteriorates and there results a lack of morality. Confucius would not be influenced by the external environment, nor tied down by the burdens of life. He maintained high moral standards and had the fortitude, great courage, and perseverance that this requires. It is precisely because of his foresight and strong sense of mission that were unabandoned, that his principles become adopted within Chinese society and set an example to be followed even today.

仁德表率

孔子不光在言语上教化自己的弟子，也以实际行动做表率：

一次，孔子路过泰山脚下，看见有一个妇人在墓前哭得很悲伤。他让子路前去问那个妇人悲伤的原因。妇人回答说："之前我的公公被老虎咬死了，后来我的丈夫又被老虎咬死了，现在我的儿子又死在了老虎口中！"孔子问："那为什么不离开这里呢？"妇人回答说："这里没有残暴的政令。"孔子说："年轻人要记住这件事，苛刻残暴的政令比老虎还要凶猛可怕啊！"

这个故事反应了孔子反对暴政，主张施行仁政的思想。他主张体察民情，爱惜民力，反对任意厮杀、鱼肉百姓。孔子虽然没有身居高位，却能体恤百姓，同情他们的遭遇，体现了他心怀大爱的思想。

还有一个小故事也体现了孔子以人为本的思想：

一次孔子家马厩失火，孔子退朝后问家人到："伤了人吗？"而并不问马的情况。孔子关心人而不关心马，这主要体现了孔子仁的主张。孔子生活在春秋战国时期，当时马比仆人或者养马的人要珍贵，地位要高，马棚着火以后，孔子先问人，而后才问马，体现了孔子一贯的"仁者爱人"思想和对人的关怀。

孔子爱人还体现在对生命的珍惜。在古代是崇尚过用活人祭祀的殉葬制度的。随着社会演变，这种惨无人道的殉葬几乎没有，逐渐改成用牲畜祭祀。到春秋时期，孔子的那个年代已经变成用陶俑替代陪葬。可就连这样，孔子也非常厌恶，他说："始作俑者，其无后乎！"意思是：那个首先作陶俑殉葬的人，是非常缺德的，他恐怕不会有后人了！

在孔子的思想中，仁是最高道德标准，是孔子毕生追求的目标。在那个礼崩乐坏的时期，国与国之间，人与人之间都由于特殊的背景而变得功利而缺失道义。孔子能够不被外部环境左右，不受生存环境所负累，时刻警记崇高的道德标准和底线，这需要极大的勇气，也需要极大的毅力。可正由于他的的高瞻远瞩和永不言弃的强烈使命感，成就了中华民族两千多年的传统美德，也成为了当今社会至今学习的榜样。

Chapter Eight

Educational Fairness

BEFORE THE SPRING AND AUTUMN period, ordinary people were not accorded an education, as it was mainly monopolised in the hands of aristocrats. There was no chance for ordinary people to go to school, so they could only engage in inferior and mundane work. Confucius, however, advocated that everybody should have an education and there should be no differences between social classes. He broke the government monopoly of learning and education. He first created a private school, giving ordinary children equal access to it. He introduced the concept of educating students according to their natural ability and applying the strategy of each one following his aspiration, which promoted educational fairness. He was the creator and pioneer of educational equality.

He recruited three thousand disciples, who came from all of the social classes, different kingdoms and from various backgrounds. For example, Yan Hui lived in a hut in a simple alley, used a bamboo to carry his rice, drank water with a ladle, was the proudest disciple of Confucius and was expected to be his successor. Zhong Gong was born in poverty, but Confucius said he could serve as the monarch of a kingdom. Zhong Gong, however, was not offered an important position and Confucius felt aggrieved for him.

Confucius not only gave those poor ordinary children the opportunity to have an equal education but also had some aristocratic disciples, such as Meng Yizi, Sima Niu, businessman Zi Gong and thief Yan Zhuoju. He thought that there should be no differences in seeking knowledge and virtue – everybody could be equal in learning, ritual, and music, and he guided them to have a higher pursuit.

Educating students according to their natural ability is the core of Confucius' ideology of educational equality. It means that different studies should be undertaken, based on the specific levels of students' interests and abilities. The following story is a good example to explain this teaching method.

One time, after class, Confucius returned to the study. His disciple Zi Lu came in and consulted him: 'Sir, if I hear a good proposal, should I immediately implement it?' Confucius looked at Zi Lu and said slowly: 'You'd better consult your father and brother before you implement it.' Just after Zi Lu left, disciple Ran You came in and respectfully asked Confucius: 'Sir, if I hear a good proposal, should I immediately carry it out?' Confucius glanced at him and immediately replied: 'Yes. You should do it at once.' After Ran You's departure, Xi Hua, who always stood by, out of curiousity asked Confucius: 'Sir, why did the same question receive an opposite reply?' Confucius smiled and said : 'Ran You is modest but hesitant, so I encouraged him to be decisive. Zi Lu is quite different, however. He is combative but incautious, so I advised him to listen more to others and act with prudence.'

Speaking out and following one's aspirations is an important component of Confucius' ideology of educational equality. He often communicated with his disciples and was honest with each. He immediately understood their situations and helped to answer their questions, leading them to build a harmonious combination of knowledge, emotion, and value. This is a democratic view of educational cognition. The following story can illustrate his teaching strategy.

Once, Confucius let his disciples talk about their aspirations. Without hesitation, Zilu said that he would like to share his horse-drawn buggy and garments with his friends. He didn't even complain about their getting worn. Yan Yuan's aspiration was not to boast of his own attributes nor to escape their drudgery for others. Confucius also said this, that is, let the elders live in peace, that friends trust each other, and the young be cared for.

In addition, Confucius also believed that teachers and students were equal. Not only those students can learn from teachers, but also vice versa. Confucius said: 'When facing an opportunity to be benevolent, one should not change even when dealing with his teacher.' Confucius said: 'In the face of benevolence, he shouldn't even be humble to his teacher.'

Confucius' 'everybody can have an education' and philosophy of educating students according to his or her natural abilities and 'speaking out and following their aspirations, teachers and students are equal' are indications of educational fairness that reflect his humanitarian spirit and embody the core of his benevolent ideology.

His educational theories still provide realistic guidance and a reference value for contemporary education that have laid the foundation for the enduring Chinese culture over more than two thousand years. Confucius broke the rule, he first reformed the educational principles, then gave ordinary people the opportunity to have an equal education, letting all the Chinese understand propriety and shame, that enables the Chinese culture to continue and endure.

公平教育

　　春秋以前，平民是没有资格入学接受教育的。教育大多垄断在贵族手中，平民很少有机会能得到教育，只能从事一些低等、粗鄙的工作。然而，孔子所倡导的"有教无类"的办学思想，打破了"学在官府"的垄断。他首创私学，使平民子弟也平等地获得了接受教育的机会。他创造的"因材施教"、"各言其志"等教学策略，有力的推动了教育公平。孔子是中国公平教育的首创者也是践行者。

　　"有教无类"的意思是，不管什么人都可以受到教育，没有等级的差别。他招收的弟子三千，来自不同诸侯国的社会阶层，拥有不同的身份背景。如颜回，身居茅屋陋巷，用竹筒子当碗盛饭，用瓢喝水，但他是孔子最得意的弟子，孔子把他当作自己的接班人。如仲弓，他出身贫寒，孔子说他有帝王之器，可以担任一国君候。后来仲弓没有得到重用，孔子还为他鸣不平。

　　孔子不光给了这些家境贫寒的平民子弟平等受教育的机会，弟子当中还有贵族子弟，如孟懿子、司马牛等，商人出身的子贡和"大盗"出生的颜涿聚等等。他认为，在求知、求德上没有高低贵贱的等级差别，任何人都应该要去接受教育，要去学习礼乐知识，并指导着他们有更高的追求。

"因材施教"是孔子教育公平思想的核心内容。意思是要针对学生的志趣、能力等具体情况进行不同的教育。下面这个典故很好的说明了孔子的"因材施教"：

有一次，弟子子路急匆匆跑来向老师请教："如果我听到一种正确的主张，可以立刻去做么？"孔子看了子路一眼，慢条斯理地说："总要问一下父亲和兄长吧，怎么能听到就去做呢？"子路刚出去，另一个学生冉有悄悄走到孔子面前，恭敬地问："先生，我要是听到正确的主张应该立刻去做么？"孔子马上回答："对，应该立刻实行。"弟子公西华一直在孔子身边，看到孔子对同一个问题有不同的回答感觉很奇怪。孔子笑了笑说："冉有性格谦逊，办事犹豫不决，所以我鼓励他临事果断。但子路逞强好胜，办事不周全，所以我就劝他遇事多听取别人意见，三思而行。"

"各言其志"则是孔子教育公平思想的重要内容。他经常与学生互动交流，坦诚相待，及时了解他们的状况，并为他们答疑解惑，从而引导他们在知识、情感和价值观上的构建。这是一种教育认知的民主观。以下这个典故可以说明孔子"各言其志"的教学策略：

有一次，孔子要学生们谈谈自己的志向。子路性子直，他说我乐意拿出自己的车马、衣服，同朋友分享，用坏了也不抱怨。

颜渊的志向是，不夸耀自己的优点，不把劳苦的事情推给别人。孔子也说出了自己的志向：让老者得到安宁，让朋友互相信任，让少者得到关怀。

此外，孔子还认为师生平等，不光是学生要向老师学，老师也应该向学生学习长处。子曰："当仁，不让于师。"—孔子说："面对仁德，就是老师也不必谦让。儒家特别强调弟子对老师的尊重，提出以孝之道侍奉师长，但孔子认为这种尊并不是盲目地服从、崇拜，而是要符合于仁道。如果师长所行与仁道违背，那么对他们也无需谦让，正如古希腊哲学家亚里士多德所说的"我爱我师，我更爱真理。"

孔子的"有教无类"、"因材施教""各言其志""师生平等"等教育公平主张，正是人道主义精神的体现，最能体现"仁"的核心思想。孔子他的公平教育至今仍对中国当代的教育有着现实的指导意义和借鉴价值，奠定了其后二千多年中华文明的兴盛。正是由于孔子打破常规，首创对教育对象的改革，实现了平民子弟也能平等受教的机会，让所有的中国人懂礼知耻，让中华文化连绵不绝、经久不衰。

Chapter Nine

Equality for All People

WHEN DISCIPLE ZHONG GONG ASKED about benevolence, Confucius answered: 'You must treat others equally'. It can be seen that treating people equally is an important aspect of Confucius' concept of 'benevolence'. Benevolence is not compassion, but respect. Compassion is often a top-down attitude that isn't heartfelt respect. Confucius asked Zhong Gong to be polite to everyone and treat them as he would a distinguished guest, regardless of whether they be a king or an ordinary person. In Confucius' eyes everyone is equal, there is no difference because of their status. He thought that a gentleman should give everyone his due, no matter who they are, and properly treat them as a guest.

The Analects recorded a story about Confucius receiving a blind musician called Mian. Possibly Mian wanted to discuss rites and music with Confucius when the latter was trying to restore the rituals of the Zhou dynasty. Confucius treated the musician with great respect. He personally escorted him. When Mian ascended the steps, Confucius told him where he was. When he came to a chair, Confucius told him to sit down. After sitting down, Confucius introduced all the guests there and told him each one's location. This was very thoughtful. After Mian left, disciple Zi Zhang asked Confucius: 'Is this the way to talk to a blind musician?' Confucius answered: 'This is the Dao of helping them and we should treat every blind person like that.'

Buddha had a blind student who wanted to sew clothes but one day couldn't find the needle eye. With sweat all over his face, he felt very anxious. Other students nearby were all busy with their work, and nobody went to help him. Buddha personally helped the blind student to thread the needle and whispered to him how to sew clothes. By demonstrating this, he told others what they should do to help all those in need. Whether a blind person or the poor, we should treat them equally without discrimination.

It can be seen that the two sages displayed the same qualities of equality and benevolence to all people. Confucius said that the virtuous man is like a great mountain that benefits all things without it being its deed. No matter whether they are big trees or small wild weeds, they can all grow.

No matter whether nobles or ordinary people, all can make use of the mountain. The mountains treat all equally, giving selflessly, having no favourites, and asking for nothing in return. Confucius said the benevolent enjoy mountains whilst the wise, water. This is because mountains and water contain deep life wisdom and the great virtue promotes growth. Only truly selfless and humanitarian people can achieve this completely. They give respect to people from the heart, understanding them, not imposing on others, or thinking from their own perspectives. They help and care for people on the basis of equality of all beings.

平等待人

当弟子仲弓问仁时,孔子告诉仲弓,一定要平等待人。可见平等待人是孔子关于什么是"仁"的一个重要内容。仁爱之心不是同情而是尊重。同情往往是从上而下的俯视,而不是发自内心的尊重。孔子要求弟子仲弓对任何人都要有礼貌、尊重,不管是对国君还是老百姓,都要如看待贵宾一样。在孔子眼里众生平等,不会因为身份贵贱而有区别,他认为君子应该一视同仁,不论是对谁都要当成贵客礼遇。

《论语.卫灵公》就记述了一个孔子接待盲人乐师的故事:有一个叫冕的盲人乐师来见孔子,也许是和孔子来探讨礼乐方面的事情吧,当时孔子正想恢复西周礼乐制度。孔子非常尊敬这位乐师,亲自为他引路。当他走到台阶边,孔子就告诉他脚下是台阶。马上到座席了,孔子就请他就坐。等坐好了,孔子又一一介绍在座的诸位并告诉他客人的方位,介绍得非常仔细。师冕走了以后,子张问孔子:"这就是和盲人乐师交谈的方式吗?"孔子说:"这就是帮助盲人乐师的道。并且说对待所有的盲人都应该这样。

释迦牟尼有一个盲人学生，有一天他想缝衣服却找不到针眼，急的满头大汗。旁边的同学们都在干着自己的事情，没有谁搭理他。这时，释迦牟尼却亲自帮这位盲学生穿好针，还轻声细语教他怎么缝衣服。他以身示范，告诉其他学生，这正是他们应该做的事情，帮助所有需要帮助的人，不管是盲人、穷人，都要一视同仁。

可见，在对人的平等和仁爱上，两位圣人都是一样的境界。孔子说有仁德的人就如同巍峨的高山，泽被万方却从不自恃己能，不论是参天大树还是杂草野花，都能在这里生长，不论是普通百姓还是王公贵族，都能到山上采取有用之物，山都一律平等对待，无私给予，从不厚此薄彼，更不求回报。

所以孔子说仁者乐山，智者乐水，是因为山水蕴含着深深的人生智慧，厚德载物。只有真正无私、真正博爱的人才能完全做到。他们会从内心尊重人、理解人，己所不欲勿施于人，他们会站在他人的角度去思考问题，在众生平等的基础上，帮助他人、关心他人。

Chapter Ten

Loving Peace

CONFUCIUS LIVED DURING THE WAR-ridden Spring and Autumn period. The states fought each other ferociously for territory and spheres of influence. They continued to annex small states, and the bigger also fought unceasingly with each other. The phenomenon of annexation, murder of kings and fathers, brothers injuring each other was very common in those days.

Confucius was totally opposed to hegemonic wars between the states. He believed those wars to be unjust, that the rulers just wanted to fulfil their own ambitions to grab wealth, land, and hegemony. There were more than forty wars between the states during the Spring and Autumn period. Confucius went around the states for 14 years in order to call for the cessation of wars. He wanted to restore the rituals of the Zhou dynasty, advocating governance by virtue, and to show concern for the conditions of people.

When disciple Zi Gong consulted Confucius about how to rule, the reply was: 'Making food sufficient, the army abundant, letting people believe in the government.' Zi Gong asked: "'If one of these elements has to be removed from the three, which should be the first?' Confucius said: 'The army first. Then the food should be removed rather than losing people's trust in the government.' It can be seen that Confucius was opposed to wars and advocated governing by virtue. Achieving prosperity for people and letting them live in stability establishes a regime- trusting people.

Ji Kangzi, who was in power in the Lu state, also asked Confucius about how to rule. He asked: 'What do you think of killing the bad people to help the good?' Confucius answered: 'Governing people doesn't need to resort to killing. The ruler's good deeds will always be followed by his people. The ruler's virtue is just like a wind, whilst that of the people is like grass. Where the wind blows, the grass will bow.' That is to say, the ruler should provide the moral lead for the people. What the ruler acts, the people will follow him.

What Confucius advocated is: 'Harmony but not uniformity'. 'All of the people within the four seas are brothers.' 'Wealth and honours attained through injustice are to me as empty as a floating cloud.' His anti-war ideas, governance by virtue and the fraternal relations between states still have a guiding significance today. This has become the origin of 'building a community with a shared future for humanity'. 'Seeking common ground while setting aside differences.' Confucius' unfinished dream is still worthy of our consideration today. We human beings should reflect on the past, and this will provide guidance for us for the future.

热爱和平

孔子生活在战火连绵的春秋时期，各诸侯国为了扩张领土和势力范围，不断吞并小国，大国之间也不断厮杀，列国兼并、弑君杀父、兄弟相残的现象十分普遍。

孔子非常反对诸侯国之间的这种倚强凌弱、以大吃小的称霸战争，他认为这类战争都是非正义的，是统治者为了满足个人攫取财富、土地、霸权的私欲，这是天下无道的表现。而春秋时期，诸侯国之间的无道战争有四十几次，孔子奔走于列国之间14年，就是要呼吁列国停止战争，恢复周朝礼制，提倡德政，体恤民情。

当子贡和孔子讨论为政之道时，孔子说，如果有充足的粮食，又有充足的军队和武器，政府就可以得到百姓的信任。子贡问："如果迫不得已要从这三项中去掉一项，那么删掉哪项呢？"孔子说去掉军队和武器。如果再去掉则宁可去掉粮食也不可缺少百姓对政府的信任。足见孔子反对战争，主张以仁德、礼义使人民归服，通过养民、富民，让人民得到安定，建立一个让老百姓信任的政权。

当鲁国位高权重的季康子问孔子如何治理政事，问："如果杀掉无道的人来成全有道的人，怎么样？"孔子说："您治理政事，哪里用得着杀戮的手段呢？您只要想行善，老百姓也会跟着行善。在位者的品德好比风，在下的百姓好比草，风吹到草上，草必随风伏倒。"（君子之德风，小人之德草，草上之风，必偃。）这是说为政者应该是百姓的道德楷模、行为榜样，他们如何做，百姓便会如何效仿。

　　孔子倡导："和而不同"，"四海之内皆兄弟"，"不义而富且贵与我如浮云"，他的反战思想，德政治国，以及国与国之间的兄弟关系，时至今日仍具有深刻的指导意义，成为了今天中国所倡导的"人类命运共同体"，"求同存异"的来源。时至今日，孔子未完成的事业依然值得我们深思，人类应该反思过去，进而指导未来。

SECTION 2 – MENCIUS

About Mencius

MENCIUS, ALSO NAMED KE, WHO lived between BC 372 and BC 289, was born in Zhou city, Shandong province. He was a famous philosopher, ideologist, educationalist, and politician who was one of the proponents of Confucianism during the Warring States period. He and Confucius are known collectively as 'Confucius and Mencius'.

Mencius inherited and developed Confucius' ideology. He developed Confucius' 'Benevolent Thought' into a political programme including politics, ideology, economy, culture, and all societal elements. He thought that 'benevolent governance' was the essential core. That is: being against wars and making proper use of the right person in politics, reducing punishment, and lowering taxes, establishing, and promoting schools in education.

He had been running after his dreams all of his life. He thought that the long years of wars were the root of people's poverty and the cause of all chaos. He advocated the suppression of class conflicts. In order to allow people to live and work in peace and contentment, he wanted to reduce the heavy taxes and distribute farmland to the farmers.

He thought that only when the king attached great importance to talent could they chose the right people to their positions. They would be happy to come and give advice on the prosperity of the state. He believed that strengthening Confucius' moral education would allow people to understand the truth of loyalty, filial piety, justice, and belief, and cultivate a philosophy of being filial to one's parents, friendly to one's brothers, loyal to one's leaders and honest in one's dealings.

孟子简介

孟子（约公元前372年—公元前289年），名轲，字子舆，邹国（今山东邹城东南）人。战国时期哲学家、思想家、政治家、教育家，儒家学派的代表人物之一，与孔子并称"孔孟"。

孟子继承并发展了孔子的思想。他继承孔子的"仁"学，把"仁"学发展成为包括政治、思想、经济、文化等各个方面的政治纲领。他认为只有实行"仁政"才是治国之本。所谓"仁政"就是在政治上反对兼并战争，要求统治者尊贤用能；经济上减轻赋税和制民之产；教育方面兴办学校，加强教育。

孟子一直在为他的"仁政"理想四处奔波。孟子还认为长年的兼并战争是造成人民生活困苦和各种祸乱的根源。他主张缓和阶级矛盾；他认为要想使人民安居乐业，必须减少繁重的赋税，把耕地和房宅基地分给农民使用；他认为国君只有重视贤才，让杰出的人都有官位，天下的贤士才会高兴而来，为国富民强出谋献策；他认为应加强儒家道德观念教育，使人们懂得忠、孝、义、信的道理，养成孝敬父母、友爱兄弟、忠于长上、办事诚实的品德。

Chapter Eleven

MENCIUS
Mencius' Mother Moved Three Times

MENCIUS' FATHER, WHO WAS NAMED Men Ji, was a scholar with much promise but with few opportunities. With great expectation, hoping to bring glory to the family name, he left home and trekked far away. He went to study in the Song state and sought an official career. Unfortunately, he couldn't realise his dream and returned home in failure. Mencius' mother had no means with which to feed her son. She made up her mind through her own efforts to provide for his food and clothes and was determined to raise her son to be a useful person in the future.

Mencius' mother was an intelligent and sensible woman who knew how to educate her children. She knew the phrase: 'If you lay down with dogs, you will end up with fleas.' In order to provide a good educational and living environment for her son, Mencius' mother moved home three times and always left with a good reputation behind her.

Mencius' family used to live near to a graveyard. Every day, undertakers were present, busy digging graves. Children in the village often saw the funerals and imitated the ceremonies. They even dug graves like the undertakers – as did Mencius.

Mencius' mother wanted her son to become a well-known scholar. She felt that the existing environment was really not fit for her son to grow up in. The only solution was to move to a better place, so they found a house near to a market. There were a lot of people there with noisy merchants showing off their goods. Mencius wandered around the market every day and was very interested in the merchandise. He learned from the merchants and promoted the goods with a loud voice.

This kind of environment was definitely not a positive influence on children, so Mencius' mother moved again, this time near to an educational institution. There were a lot of learned scholars who were polite and who acted with decorum. Exposed to this favourable environment, Mencius studied all day. Seeing this, Mencius' mother knew that this move had been the right choice this time. She felt very relieved and settled down there.

In order to provide a good study environment, Mencius' mother had moved three times. It was this devotion to the importance of education and to create a good learning environment that had provided the necessary impetus for her son and so laid a foundation for Mencius' bright future.

孟母三迁

孟子的父亲名叫孟激,是一位怀才不遇的读书人,为了更大的发展,以便光耀门楣,他抛别娇妻稚子,远赴宋国游学求仕。三年后,带给孟母的是晴天霹雳般的噩耗,从此孤立无援的孟母开始了坎坷的人生旅途。她下定决心,要凭着自己的双手谋取衣食所需,更要以自己的力量,把独生儿子教养成为一个有用的人。

孟子的母亲有见识又懂得如何教育子女,她深知"近朱者赤,近墨者黑"的道理。她为了给儿子寻找一个好的生活、学习环境,便开始了漫长的迁居活动,至今还留传有"孟母三迁"的美谈。

早年孟子一家居住在墓地附近。墓地里每天都有送葬的人忙忙碌碌,每天都有人在这里挖坟掘土。孟子和村中儿童不时看到丧葬的情形,也三五成群地模仿大人们的礼仪,扮演丧葬的过程,还常学着大人的样子拿着小铁锹挖土坑玩。

孟母一心想使儿子成为好读书、有学问的人,她感到这个环境实在不利于孩子成长,惟一的办法就是变更居住环境,于是就把家搬到集市附近。集市上人来人往、络绎不绝，行商坐贾高声叫卖，炫耀着各自的商品。孟子天天在集市上闲逛，对商人的叫卖声很感兴趣，每天都学着他们的样子，随便抓起一样东西在那里喊叫、喧闹。

这种环境对孩子更没有什么好影响了，于是孟母又把家搬到学宫附近居住。学宫是国家兴办的教育机构，聚集着很多有学问、懂礼仪的读书人。在学宫文化气氛的熏陶下，孟子也整天在家读书习礼。孟母看到这种情况，知道选对了地方，非常高兴，就在这里定居了下来。

孟子的母亲为了他有一个良好的学习环境，搬了三次家。正因为孟子妈妈重视教育，给孟子营造良好的学习氛围，对孟子进行正确的引导，为孟子的远大前程打下良好基础。

Chapter Twelve

Cutting Off the Weaving Cloth

MENCIUS, FROM THE OUTSET, EVEN as a young boy, was interested in studying. Then, after a period of time, he grew tired of it, so he started to play truant from school. Mencius' mother became very angry, picked up a pair of scissors and cut up the cloth that she had just woven. Mencius was very surprised. His mother said: 'The reason why I did this is to instruct you by use of a practical example that what you saw just now reflects the attitude that you adopt with regard to your studies. I have already woven a large piece, but it became just a wasted cloth when I cut it up. Weaving cloth should be undertaken from the beginning to the end, bit by bit, using one needle and thread. This is how your study should be. Study can't be undertaken half-heartedly. If you neglect it now, when you grow up you will end up with a job that requires hard labour, and it will be difficult to avoid disaster.'

Mencius' mother used 'cutting up the weaving cloth' as a metaphor to describe 'dropping out of school', emphasising the importance of perseverance. Once a goal has been chosen, we shouldn't be disturbed by the outside world. Things done by halves will lead to severe consequences. 'Cutting up the weaving cloth' left a deep impression on little Mencius' mind. From then on, he learned day and night and finally became a famous Confucian master in Chinese history.

断织喻学

孟子小的时候，最初对学习很有兴趣，时间一长就厌烦了，经常逃学。孟母知道后非常生气，她拿起剪刀，把刚织好的布料都给剪断了。孟子非常的吃惊，孟母说："我之所以这么做，是想通过这个真实的场景告诉你，你的学习就跟这匹布是一样的，你看前面织了那么一大段，如果说用剪刀给剪断以后就成了一块废布料了嘛，也就是说这匹布也都是从头到尾一点一滴，一丝一线的连在一起，你的学习其实也是一样的，不能说一直在努力，而中途有那么一段儿就不努力了，这样子是不行的。如果现在荒废了学业，就不免于做下贱的劳役，而且难于避免祸患。"

孟母用"断织"来警喻"辍学"，指出做事必须要有恒心，一旦认准目标，就不为外界所干扰。半途而废，后果是十分严重的。"断织喻学"的一幕在孟子小小的心灵中，留下了既惊且惧的鲜明印象，孟子从此旦夕勤学，终于成为我国历史上的儒学大师。

Chapter Thirteen

Climbing A Tree to Catch Fish

During the Warring States period, Mencius travelled from state to state teaching the principles of Confucianism. In BC 319, he visited the Qi state for the second time. At that time, the King, Qi Xuan, wished to conquer the world by military force and was preparing to attack his neighbouring state. Mencius was opposed to this, so he advised the king to abandon his war aims and adopt the policy of benevolence.

Mencius said: 'Your Majesty, why do you want to use the whole nation's army to attack other countries?' The king answered: 'To fulfil my dreams.' Then Mencius asked what the king's dream was, but the king just smiled and didn't answer. Mencius said: 'I see, Your Majesty, you want to conquer the world, do you? If you conquer the world by force, this is just like climbing a tree to catch fish. It will be impossible to achieve your goal.' The king asked: 'Is it so serious an error?' Mencius said: 'I'm afraid it is even more serious than that. Climbing a tree to catch fish is no worse than just achieving nothing but there are no severe consequences. If you use the military to satisfy your ambition of dominating the world, you will not only fail to achieve your objectives, but this will also lead to unimaginable consequences!'

The king was very surprised and asked: 'Why?' Mencius said: 'If your Majesty wishes to dominate the world by military force, bullying the weak and attacking the small, this will cause the whole world to disapprove of you and so bring disaster. If you carry out a benevolent policy, all capable hands will want to join your court to become your officials; farmers will come to plant crops on land for you; merchants will gather to your state to do business here. If you do all of this, which state has the power to act against you?'

The phrase: 'Climbing a tree to catch a fish', originally came from this episode. This means using a wrong way or choosing an opposite direction to do things that will never achieve the purpose.

缘木求鱼

战国时期，孟子周游列国，传播儒家思想。公元前319年，他第二次来到齐国。这时候，齐宣王为了扩张自己的领土，正准备攻打邻国。孟子反对战争，他劝齐王放弃武力，用仁政征服天下。

孟子说："大王动用全国军队攻打别国，这是为什么？"齐王说："为了实现我的愿望啊！"问："您最大的愿望是什么？"齐宣王却笑而不答。孟子说："那么，我明白了。您是想征服天下，是不是?如果是，我看好比爬树捉鱼，是不能达到您的目的。"齐宣王说："会有这样严重吗？"孟子说："恐怕比这还严重。爬树捉鱼，最多是捉不到，不至于有什么祸害。如果以武力满足自己独霸天下的欲望，不但达不到目的，其后果不堪设想啊！"

齐宣王吃了一惊，忙问："为什么？" 孟子说："大王想一统天下，以强欺弱，以大欺小，最后最会引起全世界所有的反对，招致祸端。如果大王能施行仁政，使天下做官的人都想到您的朝廷里来做官，天下的农民都想到您的国家来种地，天下做生意的人都想到您的国家来做生意……这样，天下还有谁能够与您为敌呢？"

成语"缘木求鱼"就是出自这里，意思是爬到树上去找鱼，它常被用来比喻做事情时如果方向、方法错误，就一定会达不到目的。

Chapter Fourteen

Sunning One Day then Freezing for the Next Ten.

WHEN MENCIUS CAME TO THE Qi state, he heard that the king was incompetent and that he had no opinions and trusted the wicked. The loyal officials in the Qi state pinned their hopes on Mencius and hoped that he could influence the king.

Mencius, did not, however, advise the king. Some complain that although Mencius knew that the king wasn't wise, he still didn't help him. Mencius explained: 'Don't think the king isn't wise enough. If it is sunny one day then freezing for the next ten, even the most robust plant cannot thrive. The time I spend with the king is limited. After I leave, the wicked will come back again to shake his resolution. Even if I could help the king to produce a few good thoughts, how could they ever last and be useful?'

Then he provided an illustration: 'There used to be a very good chess player named Yan Qiu who had two students. One was very focused on learning whilst the other was always thinking of the swan flying over the sky and of trying to shoot it with a bow. They learned together but with different results. Wasn't the second student as clever as the first? No, they were just different with regard to their levels of concentration.'

The phrase 'Sunning one day then freezing the next ten', originally came from this. This means that a person who is lacking in perseverance is always learning or working for one moment and then idling the next. It shows that everything should be done with confidence and perseverance. There will be some repeated setbacks but only one who holds to the initial motivation can achieve the goal.

一曝十寒

当孟子游说至齐国，他听说当时的齐王昏庸无能，没有主见，轻信奸佞谗言。齐国的忠臣义士得知孟子将游说齐国，倍感鼓舞，将希望寄托在孟子身上。

但孟子并未辅佐齐王。没有多久，有人责备孟子明知齐王不明智，还不辅佐他。孟子听完他们的埋怨，回答说："不要认为这是大王不够聪明。即使是天下最容易生长的植物，晒它一天，又冻它十天，它也是不能够生长的。我和大王相处的时间有限，一旦我离开大王，那些奸佞小人又来动摇大王的决心，我就算能让大王萌生一些向善的念头，又有什么用呢？"

接着，他又举例："从前有一个棋艺非常高超的人叫弈秋。弈秋有两个学生，一起跟他学习下棋，其中一个学生非常专心集中精力跟老师学习，只专心听弈秋的。另一个也在听，但心里却想着有天鹅将要从天上飞过，想拿着弓箭去射天鹅。虽然两人在一起学习下棋，第二个人却不如第一个学得好。难道是他的智力不如第一个人吗？回答：不是这样的，而是专心的程度不一样啊。"

"一曝十寒"比喻学习或工作一时勤奋，一时又懒散，没有恒心。这个成语故事，说明做任何事情都要有信心、有恒心，过程中可能会出现挫折、反复，只有坚持初心不变，才会达成目标。

Chapter Fifteen

Mencius' Three Kinds of Happiness

MENCIUS HAD THREE KINDS OF happiness. These are: parents are alive, and brothers are safe; not letting down Heaven above and Man below; being able to educate the outstanding talents in the world.

Mencius' first happiness is domestic harmony. Confucianism attaches great importance to this and thought that family rules should be placed first. They thought that the one who can't regulate the family can't govern a state. Mencius lost his father in his childhood. I believe that he used his bereavement to remind us to cherish the family and strive for domestic harmony.

Mencius' second happiness is 'not letting down Heaven above and Man below'. That is, to be 'fair and square'. How can this be satisfactory? Only living a guilt-free life with a clear conscience can make you feel free in a truthful way.

Mencius' third happiness is 'being able to educate the outstanding talents of the world'. Sharing knowledge and enlightenment with others is not only about gratitude and giving back to society but also about extending the length of life.

Mencius' three kinds of happiness really tells the true meaning of a happy life. Family harmony, self-cultivation and rewarding society are three principles that form a complete life.

The simplicity that incorporates sincerity is precious. Although Mencius' 'Three Kinds of Happiness' was written a long time ago, it is still resonant and full of wisdom. Assimilate this if you wish to achieve this happiness or you will be regret what you miss.

孟子三乐

　　孟子认为:"君子有三件快乐的事:父母健在,兄弟平安,这是第一大快乐;上不愧对于天,下不愧对于人,这是第二大快乐;得到天下优秀的人才进行教育,这是第三大快乐。"

　　这是第一件快乐的事情也就是家庭和乐。儒家非常在乎家庭和谐,认为治国先须齐家,家不齐,国不得治。孟子幼年丧父,我想他是在用自己一生的遗憾和痛楚来告诫我们:家人都健在,一定要好好珍惜。一定要和乐相处,努力做到家庭幸福。

　　孟子的第二乐:即做到"正大光明"。"岂能尽如人意?但求无愧我心",心无愧疚才能坦坦荡荡。

　　孟子的第三乐:得天下英才而教育之。与他人分享自己掌握的知识和启悟,既是感恩与回报社会,也是在薪火相传中对生命长度的延伸、对人生意义的升华。

　　平凡而质朴的"孟子三乐"的确道出了快乐人生的真谛。家庭和谐、自身修为、回馈社会,孟子眼中的三大快乐是一个立体式的架构,共同组成了一个完整的人生!

质朴的往往是真挚的，真挚的往往是珍贵的。时光虽久远，"孟子三乐"却因其质朴真挚而动人心魄，至今闪耀着智慧的光芒。也许你正拥有这些简单的快乐，珍爱并享受它们吧，如果错过了，一切就都晚了。

Chapter Sixteen

Pull up the Seedlings to Help Them Grow

THE PHRASE 'TO PULL UP the seedlings to help them grow', means 'haste makes waste'. It comes from *The Works of Mencius* and the original story reads as follows.

Once upon a time, there was a man in the Song state who was a hothead. He wanted his planted seedlings to grow faster so he went to the fields every day. One day passed, however, then two days and then three, and the seedlings still hadn't grown any higher. He said to himself: 'I have to find a way to help them grow'. Finally, he found a method. He rushed to the fields and pulled each one up. He worked for a whole day. Upon returning home, he told his family: 'I'm too exhausted but my efforts were not in vain. The seedlings have grown a lot.' His son did not understand what had happened, so he went to the field to see for himself. He saw that all the seedlings were already dead.

Pulling up the seedlings to help them grow is against the natural law. Eagerness for quick success and instant benefit without proper thinking will make things worse. The development of all things, even people's own maturation, is gradual. Whomsoever violates this rule will not just be unhelpful but also harmful.

拔苗助长

成语拔苗助长，比喻：急功近利、欲速不达。出自孟子所著作品《孟子》，原文故事如下：

从前，宋国有个急性子的农民，总嫌田里的秧苗长得太慢。他成天围着那块田转悠，隔一会儿就蹲下去，用手量量秧苗长高了没有，但秧苗好像总是那么高。用什么办法可以让苗长得快一些呢?他转啊想啊，终于想出了一个办法:"我把苗往高处拔拔，秧苗不就一下子长高了一大截吗?"说干就干，他就动手把秧苗一棵一棵拔高。他从中午一直干到太阳落山，才拖着发麻的双腿往家走。一进家门，他一边捶腰，一边嚷嚷:"哎哟，今天可把我给累坏了!"他儿子忙问:"爹，您今天干什么重活了，累成这样?"农民洋洋自得地说:"我帮田里的每棵秧苗都长高了一大截!"他儿子觉得很奇怪，拔腿就往田里跑。到田边一看，糟了!早拔的秧苗已经干枯，后拔的也叶儿发蔫，耷拉下来了。

把禾苗拔起一点，来帮助它成长，这是违反自然规律发展的，急于求成，不加思考，反而把事情弄糟。事物的发展、人的成长，都是循序渐进的，违背了这个规则不仅无益，反而有害。

Chapter Seventeen

The Fifty Laughed at the Hundred

DURING THE WARRING STATES PERIOD, wars continued year after year and caused the people to suffer greatly. Mencius travelled around from state to state in order to influence those warlike monarchs and to advocate benevolent governance. When he came to the Liang state, he met the king. The king asked: 'I tried my best to govern the state and love my people, but the population still doesn't increase, why?'

Mencius answered: 'Your Majesty, you like wars so let me apply this as a metaphor. There were two deserters who escaped from the front line during the war. One took fifty steps to escape and the other a hundred. The one who took fifty steps laughed at the one who took hundred for his incompetence. He may have taken fewer steps, but in fact both were deserters.' Then Mencius said: 'You love people, but once you wage a war and they suffer how can the population be increased? This has the same meaning as with the fifty steps man.'

King Liang Hui loved people, but he was war-like, and this situation was no different from that of the other states. Other kings may not love people as much as King Liang did, but the consequences of the wars were the same. They would all lead to injury and death, so the population decreased. They were just at a different level but essentially the same in terms of the people suffering.

The phrase 'The fifty laugh at the hundred' as used in China has the same meaning as that of 'The pot calling the kettle black' in English. This was used as a metaphor to describe something that is essentially the same but at a different level. The story also reflected the political thoughts of Mencius in advocating benevolent governance, propriety, being against wars and hegemony.

五十步笑百步

战国时期，战争连年不断，苦了各国的老百姓。孟子看了，决定周游列国，去劝说那些好战的君主施行仁政。孟子来到梁国，去见了好战的梁国。梁惠王对孟子说："我费心尽力治国，又爱护百姓，却不见百姓增多，这是什么原因呢？"

孟子回答说："大王喜欢战争，那就让我用战争作比喻吧。有两个士兵在前线打仗时败下来，一个逃跑了五十步，另一个逃跑了一百步，逃跑了五十步的耻笑逃跑了一百步的不中用。他们只是逃跑的远近不同罢了，其实都是逃跑啊。"孟子又说："您虽然爱百姓，可你喜欢打仗，一打仗，百姓还是要遭殃，又怎么会增加呢？这与五十步同理。"

梁惠王虽然爱民，但他"好战"，与其他临国之政并无太大区别。其他的国王虽不爱民，但打仗的后果是一样的，只是程度稍微轻些而已，本质上老百姓都遭殃。（就人民遭受痛苦的本质而言）

"五十步笑百步"通常用来比喻"自己跟别人有同样的缺点或错误，只是程度上轻一些，可是却指责嘲讽别人。这个成语也表达了孟子主张王道，提倡礼乐，反对霸道，反对战争的政治理念。

Chapter Eighteen

Benevolence Is Invisible

King Liang Hui said: 'You know that the Wei state is the strongest country in the world. During the time of my reign, I was defeated in the east by the Qi state and my eldest son was killed during the course of this. I lost seven hundred parts of my territory to the Qin state in the west. I was humiliated by the Chu state in the south. I am very ashamed by all of this and would love to wash away all the hate for the dead, but how can I do so?'

Mencius replied: 'A hundred miles of land can allow one to become a king. Your Majesty, if you rule the people with benevolent governance – reduce punishment, lower taxes, allow the people to work on their farms, have time to cultivate a filial, respectful, loyal, and trustworthy character so they can show respect and obedience to parents and brothers in the family, and respect their elders and leaders – then they can confront those Qin and Chu armies even with wooden sticks. Those Qin and Chu states are deprived of people's productive time so they can't do farm work and be filial. Their parents are cold and hungry, their wives and brothers separated from them. This causes people to live in hell. Which state has the power to act against you if you adopt benevolent governance? Benevolence is natural, so please don't hesitate!'

Mencius believed that only benevolent governance was the right approach. He had been promoting this ideal all of his life. He thought that the long years of wars were the root of people's poverty and the cause of all chaos. In politics, he was against wars and advocated making proper use of the appropriate people. In economics, he attempted to reduce sanctions and taxes. In education, he called for the establishment of schools and the promotion of education. He believed that people would support their king if there were a benevolent government so they would have one mind. Many hands make light work, so the benevolence is seamless.

仁者无敌

梁惠王说："魏国是天下最强的国家，你是知道的。到了我这一代，东面战败于齐国，长子阵亡；西面丧失了七百里疆土给秦国；南面受辱于楚国。我对此感到耻辱，愿意替死者来洗刷所有的仇恨，怎样才能办到呢？"

孟子答道："拥有方圆百里的土地就能称王天下。大王如果对老百姓施行仁政，减免刑罚，少收赋税，深耕细作，及时除草；让身强力壮的人抽出时间修养孝顺、尊敬、忠诚、守信的品德，在家侍奉父母兄长，出门尊敬长辈上级.这样就是让他们制作木棒也可以打击那些拥有坚实盔甲锐利刀枪的秦楚军队了。因为那些秦国、楚国的执政者剥夺了他们老百姓的生产时间，使他们不能够深耕细作来赡养父母。父母受冻挨饿，兄弟妻子东离西散。他们使老百姓陷入深渊之中，大王去征伐他们，有谁来和您抵抗呢？所以说：'施行仁政的人是无敌于天下的。'大王请不要疑虑！"

孟子认为只有实行"仁政"才是治国之本。孟子一直在为他的"仁政"理想四处奔波。孟子还认为长年的兼并战争是造成人民生活困苦和各种祸乱的根源。他认为所谓"仁政"就是在政治上反对兼并战争，要求统治者尊贤用能；经济上减轻赋税；教育方面兴办学校，加强教育，培养品德。他认为施行仁政的君王，必然赢得民众的拥戴；上下一心，众志成城，是无敌于天下的。

SECTION 3 – Lao Zi

About Lao Zi

LAO ZI, WHOSE FAMILY NAME was Li and surname Er, was born during the late Spring and Autumn period. He was born around 571 BC, in Ku County in the Chu state (historians commonly believed that Ku County is Lu Yi in today's Henan province). He was the Chinese creator of the Daoist philosophy, and an ancient thinker, philosopher, writer, and historian.

It is said that he was born with white eyebrows and beard, and so people called him Lao Zi. He was intelligent and studious from an early age. He first became a disciple of Shang Rong, who was skilled in the rituals and music of the Zhou dynasty. Three years later, he went to the capital of Zhou state to study. Later, he became the curator of the national museum and library of the Zhou state and was well known for his knowledge at that time.

The core of Lao Zi's theory was through his dialectical views that deeply influenced the development of Chinese philosophy and religion. He advocated the use of non-action and of teaching without words.

The *Dao De Jing* was Lao Zi's famous work that is also called *Lao Zi*. According to UNESCO, besides the Bible, it is the most widely published book in the world.[1]

---

[1] See our previous book – Dao de Jing

Lao Zi's work and thoughts have become an important contribution to the world's historical and cultural heritage. By the 1940s and 1950s, there were more than 60 different translations of the *Dao De Jing* in Europe. Many famous scholars, such as the German philosophers Hegel and Nietzsche, and the Russian writer Tolstoy deeply studied the *Dao De Jing* and so wrote books and essays about it.

老子简介

老子，姓李名耳，是春秋末期人，约公元前571年出生于楚（原为陈）国苦县（史学界普遍认为今河南省鹿邑县）。中国古代思想家、哲学家、文学家和史学家，道家学派创始人和主要代表人物。

相传老子一生下来就是白眉毛白胡子，所以人们就叫他老子。老子自幼聪慧好学，他先是拜精通殷商礼乐的商容老先生为师，三年后他入周都深造，后担任东周国都洛邑担任守藏史这一职位，这就相当于我们现在的国家图书馆馆长，以其学识渊博闻名遐迩。

老子思想对中国哲学发展具有深刻影响，其思想核心是朴素的辩证法。在社会治理上，老子主张无为而治、不言之教。在管理上，老子讲究物极必反之理。在修身方面，老子讲究虚心实腹、不与人争的修持。

老子传世作品《道德经》（又称《老子》），据联合国教科文组织统计，《老子》一书是当今除《圣经》外，在全世界出版发行数量最多的一本书。

老子的著作、思想已成为世界历史文化遗产的宝贵财富。到二十世纪四五十年代，欧洲共有 60 多种《道德经》译文，德国哲学家黑格尔、尼采，俄罗斯大作家托尔斯泰等世界著名学者对《道德经》都有深入的研究，并都有专著或专论问世。

Chapter Nineteen

LAO ZI
The Origin of the *Dao De Jing*

ABOUT 485 BC, LAO ZI, UPON seeing that the Zhou dynasty was becoming more and more corrupt, became very despondent. He decided to leave his hometown, and riding on a blue bull he travelled west to the Hangu Pass, wandering all across the terrain.

The official of the frontier was named Yin Xi. One day, when he was standing by the gate of the city, he saw a purple cloud flying from the east. Yin Xi was a learned person so he knew that there must be a sage coming.

The purple cloud indicated that a sage would pass through the city gate, so he waited there in anticipation. Later, an extraordinary and charming elder, who looked sage-like and was riding a blue bull, slowly came towards the gate. Recognising him as Lao Zi, Yin Xi, who deeply admired his wisdom, felt great pity for the sage. He asked him to stay but was unable to change Lao Zi's mind. Yin Xi asked Lao Zi to write a book that would benefit future generations and thereby leave his name to posterity. This was the origin of the *Dao De Jing*.

The book was based on the rise and fall of a dynasty that took people's safety for granted and caused disaster and was thus intended as a warning. The original version was divided into two parts. These comprised some five thousand words.

The first thirty-seven chapters are called 'Dao Jing'. The remaining forty-four chapters (from thirty-eight to eighty-one) are the second part and are known collectively as 'De Jing'. The 'Dao Jing' talks about the root of the universe and describes the changes of Heaven and Earth and the subtlety of Yin and Yang. 'De Jing' talks about dealing with the circumstances and of the world that contains the eternal essence of Dao.

As if discovering a treasure, Yin Xi diligently studied it all day long. Lao Zi rode on his blue bull again; after leaving the great 'five thousand words' work, he retreated into privacy –legend states that it was to Jinshi Mountain, later renamed Lao Zi Mountain.

《道德经》的由来

大约周敬王三十五年（公元前485年），老子看到周王朝越来越衰败，他感到非常失望，于是他骑上青牛，准备离开故土，西出函谷关，四处云游。

把手函谷关的长官叫尹喜。这一天他正站在城关上了望着，只见关谷中有一团紫气从东方冉冉飘移过来。关令尹喜是一个修养与学识极其高深的人。他一看到这种气象，心里一顿，这是有圣人来了！只有圣人来才会有这样的云气，今天一定有圣人要经过我的城关了，不知是哪一位。不多一会儿，就见到一位仙风道骨的人，骑着一头青牛慢慢向关口行来。竟然是老子！尹喜很敬佩老子，他对于老子的离去非常惋惜，他想留住老子但无法改变老子的决定，于是就请老子留下一部著作流芳百世、造福后代。这就是道德经的由来。

这篇著作以王朝兴衰成败、百姓安危祸福为鉴，溯其源，著上、下两篇，共五千言。上篇为前37章称《道经》。下篇从38章开始，称《德经》，一共是81章。《道经》言宇宙本根，含天地变化之机，蕴阴阳变幻之妙；下篇《德经》，言处世之方，含人事进退之术，蕴长生久视之道。

尹喜得之，如获至宝，终日默诵，如饥似渴。老子留下这部"五千言"伟大著作后，就骑着大青牛走了，相传归隐修炼于景室山（后更名为"老君山"）。

Chapter Twenty

The Dao of Lao Zi

THE *DAO DE JING* HAS become popular the world over. What does 'Dao' really mean to people? It seems very profound and hard to understand. The word 'Dao' crops up 73 times in the *Dao De Jing*, but does it have a consistent meaning?

The fact is that Dao appears many times in the chapters, but the meaning is not always the same. The three main meanings of Dao can be summarised here as follows.

To begin with, the term Dao stands for metaphysical existence. It has the characteristic of metaphysics in that it is both invisible and indescribable, but it is really just existence. For example: 'The Dao that can be expressed as thus is not the Eternal Dao; the name that can be expressed as thus is not the eternal name. True Dao is beyond words and cannot be expressed conceptually, so, reluctantly, we give it a name for convenience. Lao Zi thought that Dao was the root of all existence that produces everything. It raises and cultivates those that possess infinite potential and creativity.

Secondly, Dao is a rule. It is invisible, but when it is used in all things it follows some laws. For example, Lao Zi believed that all phenomena were also formed in the opposite state: existence and nothingness, difficult and easy, long, and short. The value of a human being's existence is also relative: everyone in the world learns beauty as is, thus ugliness exists; everyone in the world learns goodness as is, thus evil exists. He further shows that the opposite state can mutually transform misfortune may be a blessing in disguise and vice versa. There are natural laws: 'a fierce wind cannot last a whole morning and intense rainfall cannot continue for a whole day'. 'Softness overcomes rigidity' and so on.

Thirdly, Dao is the rule of life. To the lover of life, it is an indicator of human behaviour that becomes the way of life and of how to operate. This Dao has the same meaning as 'De', such as 'retire after achieving merit, this is the natural law'. Dao here contains the meaning of 'modesty' and 'non-competition'. In this sense, Dao is the same as Dethat can be followed by human beings.

The development of Lao Zi's philosophical system could be said to extend from cosmology to the theory of life and then to politics. The central idea of his philosophy is Dao and the whole system that is carried out around it was predetermined. The five-thousand-word *Dao De Jing* contains infinite wisdom. As German philosopher Nietzsche said: 'like an inexhaustible well that is full of treasure'.

老子的"道"

《道德经》风靡世界,老子的"道"到底是什么意思呢?仿佛高深莫测,玄机深远。书中73次提到的"道",他们都是同一个意思吗?

原来,老子的"道"虽然在不同章节中多次出现,但字相同,意义却有不同。在此,我总结归纳《道德经》中的"道"的三种不同含义:

一、"道"是形而上的实存。"道"具有形而上的性格,它的不可名,就是由于它的无形,但却是真实的存在。如"道可道,非常道;名可名,非常名。"真实的"道"是不可言说的,无法用概念来表达,勉强称之为"道",只是为了方便称呼。老子认为,道是一切存在的根源,"道"产生天地万物,畜养他们,培育它们,具有无穷的潜在力和创造力。

二、"道"是一种规律。"道"虽无形,然作用于万物时,却展示了某种规律。如:老子认为一切现象都是在相反对立的状态下形成的:有无相生、难易相成、长短相形等;人间的存在价值也是相对而生的:天下皆知美之为美,斯恶已;皆知善之为善，斯不善已；他进一步说明相反对立的状态是相互转化的，如：祸兮福之所倚，福兮祸之所伏；还有自然规律"飘风不终朝，骤雨不终日。""柔弱胜刚强"等等。

三、"道"是生活准则。"道"落实到生活层面，则作为人间行为的指标，成为人类的生活方式与处事方法了，这层意义上的"道"就是"德"，它们意义相同。如"功遂身退，天之道也。"这里的"道"蕴含着"谦退""不争"的精神，这层意义上，"道"同于"德"，落实到人生层面，可以为人类去效法。

老子整个哲学系统的发展，可以说是由宇宙论伸展到了人生论，再由人生论延伸到了政治论。他哲学的中心观念就是"道"，他的整个哲学系统都是由他所预设的"道"而开展的。五千言的《道德经》蕴含了无穷的智慧。借用德国哲学家尼采所说："像一个永不枯竭的井泉，载满宝藏。"

Chapter Twenty-One

Non-Interference

BEING NATURAL AND NOT INTERFERING are Lao Zi's two most important tenets. He believed that everything should work in its own natural way. Do not interfere with things using external force and so avoid violating the natural law.

Lao Zi promoted the belief that the seeming contradictions within human society are actually complementary and symbiotic. Everything has two sides, Nothingness and Existence co-exist. Difficult and easy complement each other. Long and short describe each other. High and low show each other. Sound and voice harmonise with each other. Front and back follow each other.

Lao Zi advocated following the path of Heaven and Earth to let all things develop without interference. Heaven doesn't interfere with them nor claim credit for the accomplishment.

Heaven and Earth have great beauty, but they never speak; seasons have obvious differences, but they never criticise; all things are created by their own causes, but they never talk. The sage should praise the beauty of Heaven and Earth, understand the truth of all things so that he acts without interference, just complying with the natural law.

Lao Zi said: 'A fierce wind, therefore, cannot last a whole morning. Intense rainfall cannot continue for a whole day. Even Heaven and Earth cannot prevail for long, so how could a human being?' Lao Zi advocated complying with the natural law. If executive orders are complicated and burdensome, then they are just like the fierce wind and intense rainfall and will not endure, thus they will cause harm to people. Tyranny cannot last long because it doesn't act according to the natural law.

Lao Zi also said that all things have their own nature. Some go ahead whilst some follow behind. Some are slow whilst some are hasty. Some are strong whilst others are weak. Some are self-loving whilst some are self-destructive. The world is sacred and cannot be interfered with and controlled by force. He who interferes with it by force will lose it. He who controls it by force will lose it. Everything should follow human rules according to the situation; act without interference and get rid of all extreme actions.

Two thousand years ago, when Lao Zi was living through turbulent times, he was concerned about the rulers whose 'self-righteous interference with others' fates' was causing disaster. It was the ruler running amok that led to injustice and cruelty amongst humanity. If the ruler could be without desire, applying the principle of non-action and letting people develop freely, they would be able to fulfil themselves, so that they could live in harmony, safety, and prosperity. Society would be in a harmonious, stable, and unified state. This is the ultimate goal. Lao Zi's wish for a society of natural being and non-action still has a significance and resonance in today's world.

勿干涉

自然无为是老子哲学的一个重要观点，老子认为任何事物都应该顺应它自身发展的情况，不应该用外力去干涉，违背事物发展的自然规律。

老子认为人类社会的矛盾都是相辅相生，相互转换的，有无相生，难易相成，长短相形，高下相盈，音声相和，前后相随。他主张效法天道，顺应自然，就像万物自然生长，老天不加干预，不据为己有，不自恃己能。统治者也应当少发政令，遵从自然，不要扰民，应该化解和转换天下万物的矛盾，最好的政府是人民感觉不到政府的干预，这样人类社会也永远地和谐统一。

天地有大美，然而却不言语；四时有明显的季节，却从不议论；万物有生成的道理，然而从不说话。圣人遵从天地的大美，通达万物的道理，所以他们无为，只是效法天地的自然法则而已。

老子说："狂风刮不到一早晨，暴雨下不了一整天。兴起风雨的天地都无法持久，何况于渺小的人类呢？"所以老子说要效法自然，效法天道。如果政令繁苛，就犹如这狂风骤雨，对人民造成侵害，也就不能持久。暴政不能持久，就是由于不合于自然的缘故。

老子还说，世间万物都有天性，有的积极，有的消极，有的性缓，有的性急，有的强健，有的羸弱，有的自爱，有的自毁。天下神器，不能出于强力，不能加以把持。想要治理天下却用强力去做，是达不到目的的。出于强力的一定失败，强加把持的，一定会失去。因此凡事应当遵循人情，依势而为，效法自然无为而治，除去一切极端过分的措施。

两千多年前，老子处于那样动乱的时代，深深感觉到那些自以为是想成为他人命运主宰者给百姓带来的灾难，统治者的胡作非为造成了人间的不平和残暴的根源。如果为政者能做到无欲、无为，让人民自由发展、自我完成，那么人民能够自由自在，平安富足，使社会归于自然和谐，安定统一，这就是一个理想的大同社会了。老子提出的自然无为的梦想社会，在现实看来仍具有其时代的意义和生命力。

Chapter Twenty-Two

Gentleness Overcomes Strength

IN LAO ZI'S PHILOSOPHY, THERE is one very important tenet. This is that gentleness overcomes strength. Lao Zi often used water as a metaphor, as he thought that it is the gentlest object. Running water dropping from mountains can break through stones; floods can swamp farmland and houses. There is nothing gentler than water, but it has a most powerful energy. Nothing can resist it. Where did this view come from? It came from his teacher's enlightenment.

Lao Zi's teacher, Chang Cong, once wished to test his pupil. He asked: 'Look at my tongue, is it still there?' Lao Zi answered: 'Of course, it is there.' Then his teacher asked: 'What about my teeth?' Lao Zi smiled and said: 'They disappeared a long time ago.' The teacher continued with his questions: 'Do you know why this is so?' Lao Zi said: 'The tongue exists because the softest can easily survive. The teeth have fallen out because they are too hard.'

The tongue is flexible. It will retract if it touches hot or hard objects. Teeth, however, always confront the tough with toughness. When people are old, the soft tongue is still there but the teeth may have fallen out[2]. Lao Zi was inspired by this and began to study the

---

[2] Please note that this was written thousands of years ago when dentistry was not quite optimal

phenomenon, so he came up with this tenet. Lao Zi added: 'When we are alive, the body is soft but after death, it will turn to hardness. When vegetation flourishes, it is soft but after decay, it will dry up.' He concluded that the hard belongs to the category of death, but the soft to that of survival.

When Lao Zi lived during those war-ridden times, the states fought each other fiercely for hegemony. He wanted people to be friendly and live in harmony. He hoped that the states would stop fighting and eliminate disputes. Through 'non-action' everything runs its own course. This is in harmony with the natural law.

柔弱胜刚强

在老子的道家思想里，有个很重要的观点是柔弱胜刚强。老子常拿水来作比喻，他认为水最为柔弱，但高山上的流水长年累月可以能够穿破石头，洪水泛滥能够淹没农田和房屋。天下没有比水更柔弱的事物了，但它却蕴含着天下最强大的力量，任何坚固的东西都抵挡不了。这就是他柔弱胜刚强的思想，那么，他的这个思想从哪里来呢？原来是起源于老师对他的教诲。

老子的老师叫常枞，一次常枞想考一考老子，他问："你看，我的舌头还在吗？"老子说："当然还在。"常枞又问："我的牙齿还在吗？"老子笑了："早就没有了。"常枞紧接着问老子："你知道原因是什么吗？"老子回答说："那舌头之所以存在,是因为它很柔软得以生存,牙齿不存在,是因为它太刚硬所以掉光了"。

舌头天性灵活自如，碰到硬的烫的都会躲开，牙齿却总是硬碰硬。所以人老了，柔软的舌头还在，坚硬的牙齿却掉光了。老子从中受到了启发，开始用心观察和研究这种现象，终于得出了规律。老子还告诉人们人活着的时候，身体是柔弱的，死了以后就变得坚硬了。草木欣欣向荣的时候是柔弱的，衰败以后就变得干枯了。所以他得出结论，说明坚强的东西属于死亡一类，柔弱的东西属于生存一类。

在老子所处的时代，战火纷飞，列强争霸，他希望人与人之间要保持友好关系，和谐相处，国与国之间不要争霸，消除争端，应该无为而治，顺乎自然，符合天道。

Chapter Twenty-Three

The Value of Nothingness

IN LAO ZI'S PHILOSOPHY, 'EXISTENCE and nothingness' often appear together, as pairs. Their relationship is full of subtlety that reflects the unique nature of the Daoist philosophy. In our minds, having something, obviously, is more valuable than nothing, such as having money and power, and so on. In Daoist philosophy, comparing with 'existence', Lao Zi and Zhuang Zi placed more emphasis on the value and function of 'nothingness'. Why?

Lao Zi believed that existence is just a current benefit whilst nothingness can really transcend. He said that when somebody moulds clay to make a vessel it is empty, and this creates the usable space. If it is solid, it isn't functional at all but merely decoration.

It is the vessel's empty space (nothingness) that is the most useful. He also includes that somebody excavates a door and windows to build a room. The room is empty, so this provides the space to be occupied. If it is full, then it isn't functional at all so the house's empty space (nothingness) is the crucial component.

Chuang Zi inherited and developed Lao Zi's theory. Once, Chuang Zi's good friend Huizi complained about a useless big tree. The tree was very big, but it was crooked and irregular so even a carpenter wouldn't take a second glance at it. Huizi thought that it was really an insignificant tree.

Zhuang Zi said that this was the function of nothingness. Just because of its uselessness, it cannot be cut down by an axe or be damaged by external objects. This is the advantage of uselessness! Besides, in the boundless fields, it creates a shade for people to lie down under and enjoy the cool in summer, so isn't it comfortable and free?

Daoism promotes the belief that, in a society that has no sense of right or wrong, this will result in aggression and competition. Valuing uselessness is an approach that results in longevity. If everything works in its own natural way, there will be less confrontation in society. If there is no competition, people live and work in peace and contentment. The whole world will be united.

无的用处

在道家思想中，"有和无"常常是成对出现，他们的关系充满奥妙，这也体现了道家思想的独到之处。在我们通常的观念中，显然"有"更有价值，比如有钱、有势、有权。但在道家思想中，相对于"有"，老子和庄子更强调"无"的作用和价值。为什么呢？

老子认为，"有"只是一种存在的利益，"无"才发挥作用。他说：有人用陶土作成瓦罐，但是罐子只有空心的时候才有用，如果罐子是实心的，就没有一点作用，只能摆看。

所以正是罐子的"无"在发挥作用。他还说，造一间房子，房子里面必须是空的，才能给人居住，这就是"无"的作用。如果里面是有东西的，是满的，房子就发挥不了作用。

庄子继承和发扬了老子的思想。

一次，庄子的好朋友惠子抱怨说，他看到一颗大树，弯弯曲曲，也不规整，木匠看都不愿看一眼。没有一点作用。

庄子却说，这就是无用的用处啊，正因为无用所以它不会被斧头砍伐，不会被外物伤害。这就是无用的好处啊！况且，在空旷无边的田野上，它可以营造一片荫庇之所，夏日时逍遥自在的躺在树下纳凉岂不自在？

在是非不明，权力角逐的社会里，道家认为无用之用是得以保全天寿的一种途径。当一切顺从于自然，万物合为一体，人伦社会的违法乱纪自然就没有了，人世间没有了争斗，人人得以安居乐业，企盼的大同世界也就来临了。

Chapter Twenty-Four

The Highest May Have a Fall

THERE ARE TWO THINGS IN the world that are the most difficult to fill: one is the sea, and the other is desire. The sea is hard to fill because of its vastness and openness. Desire is hard to fill because human nature is greedy and ugly. Two thousand years ago, Lao Zi pointed out that life should be reasonable. The highest may have a fall, everything reaches its pinnacle and then is bound to decline. All things must be measured – too much water drowned the miller.

Lao Zi believed that everything alternates repeatedly to and from the opposite state and that this cycle is endless. He said: 'Misfortune may be a blessing in disguise and vice versa.' There is a famous idiom called 'blessing in disguise' that says happiness and disaster change into and depend on each other.

A poor old man lived on the northern border of China. One day, his stallion ran north of the China border into the land of the northern tribes, later to be known as Mongolia. In the old days, a horse was one of the most valuable things to own, so the other villagers thought this was a very bad misfortune.

The old man did not worry, and he thought that this may actually be a blessing. A few months later, the old man's horse returned with a mare. The mare was pregnant and gave birth to a foal. Now all the villagers congratulated the old man, but he thought that this may actually turn out to be a cause of misfortune.

Later his son fell off the horse and was crippled for life. When the villagers comforted him, he said: 'Perhaps this will turn out to be a blessing'. One year later, the northern tribes launched a major invasion into China. All able-bodied young men were required to fight against the invaders. Nine out of ten men were dying in battle. Since the father was old and his son was crippled, neither were required to go to war and both survived.

Sometimes life's misfortunes are more than one would expect; we should adjust our mentality and deeply understand the nature of things.

Why did Lao Zi attach great importance to the state and transformation of, and to, the opposite side? He believed that things were produced by the opposite relationship. He wanted to awaken people to see the positive from the negative in order to understand the profound meaning behind it. He thought the highest may have a fall.

He said: 'Letting a cup overflow rather than stopping it in time. Sharpening a sword to its sharpest so that it will not last. Rigidity is easily broken. Don't be too proud, and allow for unforeseen circumstances. The Way of Heaven is to diminish superabundance and to supplement deficiency. Knowing this, we should nip cries in the bud, be modest even if we have outstanding achievement, be self-effacing even we are talented. Retire after achieving merit. This is the natural law.

物极必反

世界上有两种东西是最难填满的,一个是大海,一个是欲望,大海填不满是因为它博大而包容,欲望填不满是因为人性的贪婪与丑恶。早在两千多年前的《道德经》中,老子就指出人生讲求一个度字,物极必反、物壮则老,凡事须有度,过犹而不及。

老子认为一切事物都是在对立相反的状态中反复交替着,这种反复转化的过程是无止尽的。他说:"祸兮,福之所倚;福兮,祸之所伏。"中国有个著名的成语故事叫"塞翁失马焉知非福",说的就是福祸相互转换,相依相生的道理。

边塞地方住着一个人,有一天他家的马无缘无故跑到胡人那里去了,大家都安慰他。他父亲说:"这怎么就知道不是福气呢?"过了几个月,他家的马带着胡人的骏马回来了,人家都祝贺他。他父亲说:"这怎么就知道不是祸患呢?"家里多了良马,他的儿子喜欢骑马,有一次从马上摔下来折断了大腿骨,大家都安慰他,他的父亲又说:"这怎么就知道不是福气呢?"过了一年,胡人大举侵入边塞,壮年男子都拿起弓箭参战,住在边塞附近的壮年男子百分之九十的人都因战争而死去,因为他儿子腿瘸的原因，父子的性命都得以保全。谁知道是福还是祸呢？所以无论遇到福还是祸，要调整自己的心态，深刻认识事物的本质。

　　老子为什么这么重视事物相反对立的状态和对立面的转化呢？老子认为事物是在对立关系中产生的，他想唤醒大家从反面关系中来看正面，以认识正面的深刻涵义。他认为万事万物，一到强壮盛大的时候，就开始趋于衰败，发展到极致都必然走下坡路，这就是物极必反的道理。他说"水满则溢，不如适时停止。显露锋芒，不能长久保持，过于刚强容易折损。人不要自满，要藏而不露。"天之道，损有余而补不足。了解到这种盛极而衰的道理后，对于很多事情要防患于未然，即便功勋卓著也要懂得谦虚，即便才华横溢也要懂得韬光养晦。功遂身退，天之道也。

Chapter Twenty-Five

Stillness and Peace

STILLNESS AND PEACE MEAN THAT all distractions, such as desires and rational thoughts, should be dispelled to attain peace and purity of the soul. The idea was first proposed by Lao Zi.

We usually use the term 'a deep and broad valley' as a metaphor to describe a modest attitude. Lao Zi said: 'The sage's mind is like a bellows or a valley that is boundless, endless, and inexhaustible, so he will never be full of himself. The sea is vast and can contain all rivers so it can be itself.'

The reverse side of the void is full. Lao Zi said: 'Letting a cup overflow rather than stopping it in time; sharpening a sword to its sharpest will not endure. Too hard is easily broken so don't be complacent but hide your sources.'

Facing the complexities of the world, Lao Zi hoped that people would maintain stillness and peace. He advocated that this principle, to keep quiet and adopt non-interference, would become the guide for the world. Governing a state is like cooking a small fish. You cannot turn it, or it will be easily broken. Lao Zi used to cook a small fish as a metaphor to describe governing a state that means keeping to stillness and peace as a principle and not to interfere with people.

It is not only in ruling a state that one should keep quiet and adopt non-interference but also in a man's life. He opposed the pursuit of sensory pleasures and awakened people to the notion of seeking stillness to temper desires. He let people be quiet in their busy time, centre themselves and subdue the activity with stillness. Once the human spirit enters into an extreme calm state without desires, is there any vexation that can remain? Can everything be resolved and be natural?

虚静

虚静是排除一切欲望与理性的干扰，达到心灵的纯净与安宁。这个概念最先由老子提出，他说："致虚极，守静笃"，他认为万物的本源就是虚静的状态。

我们常用虚怀若谷来形容胸怀像山谷那样深且宽广，形容十分谦逊的人。老子说：圣人的胸怀就得好像天地间的风箱，又好似山间的低谷，无边无际、绵绵若存、用之不竭，所以从不会自满。大海浩瀚无边，因为它能包容一切河流，所以成其为大海。

虚的反面也就是满。老子又说："水满则溢，不如适时停止。显露锋芒，不能长久保持，过于刚强容易折损。人不要自满，要藏而不露。"

面对世事的复杂纷扰，老子希望人世间能够持守虚静。老子主张为政应该清静，清静为天下正。治理国家就像是煎小鱼一样，不能常常翻动它，多翻则易碎。老子用煎小鱼来比喻治理国家，意思是要以清静为原则，不可以扰民。

不仅为政清静，人的一生也应该持守虚静。他反对追求声色享乐，唤醒大家在多欲中求清静。要人在繁忙中静下心来，在急躁中稳定自己、以静制动、以逸待劳。人的精神进入一种无欲无求失无功利的极端平静的状态，那么世事还有什么烦恼？不都能够迎刃而解、一任自然了吗？

Chapter Twenty-Six

Abstain from Military Force

WARS HAVE BROUGHT GREAT DISASTERS to mankind. Lao Zi expressed his anti-war philosophy and aversion to conflict. He thought that a follower of Dao shouldn't try to conquer the world by military force. Such a course is sure to meet an equivalent response. There is no good end to wars, wherever the military goes, briar and thorns will take root. After a war, corpses are everywhere, and plagues spread. A year of death is sure to follow a great war.

Firstly, the attitude of aversion to wars. Lao Zi believed that weapons were evil tools that were hated by all people. A man of the Dao shouldn't quickly resort to military force.

Secondly, even if it is necessary to use military force, one shouldn't rely upon it. Lao Zi also knew that some wars were inevitable so if there was a need to use military force, this should be for a limited purpose and then quickly cease. Do not indulge in aggressive wars and love violence.

Thirdly, even in victory, there is no pride or joy. A victory in a war should be regarded like that of a funeral rite. The slaughter of multitudes should attract sorrow and be mourned. Don't get carried away with enthusiasm for a victory. He who is joyful is proud of killing and won't be successful in the world.

Lao Zi said: 'He who relies on the power of force will be lost. When trees reach full growth, they will be cut down. Indulging in aggressive wars will lead only to ruin. Sharp weapons of the state should be left where none can see them. The highest may have a fall. Things become old after reaching their prime.' Lao Zi's attitude to wars is still of great significance to this day.

戒用兵

战争会给人类带来巨大的灾祸，老子在《道德经》中表达了他的反战思想和对战争的厌恶情绪。他认为有道的国君是不会用兵力征服天下的。用武力征服他国必遭报复。战争是没有好下场的，军队所到之处，荆棘丛生，每次大战之后，尸横片野、瘟疫传播，必定是一个灾荒之年。

第一，厌恶战争的态度。老子认为兵器是不祥的东西，人们都厌恶它，有道的人不会轻言战事。

迫不得已用兵不可逞强。老子也知道有些战争不可避免，迫不得已才用兵。万不得已用兵的话达到目的就可以了，不可以穷兵黩武逞强好战。

第三，胜之不美，丧礼处之。战争中杀人众多，要用哀痛的心情参加。即便打了胜仗，也要以丧礼来对待，不可以得意忘形。得意就是喜欢杀人，喜欢杀人，不可得志于天下。

老子说：用兵逞强就会遭受灭亡，树木强大就会遭受砍伐。凡是用兵力来逞强天下的，最终都是自取灭亡。"国之利器不可以示人"，物极必反、物壮则老，老子对待战争的态度对当今的后世仍有深刻的指导意义。

SECTION 4 – Zhuang Zi

About Zhuang Zi

ZHUANG ZI, WHOSE FAMILY NAME was Zhuang and given name Zhou, was a thinker, philosopher, and writer. He was born during the Warring States period and his ancestor was the emperor of the Song state. He was the successor figure to Lao Zi and founded an important philosophical school known as the Zhuang School. Zhuang Zi and Lao Zi were together known as Lao Zhuang.

Zhuang Zi would not accept the position offered by the Emperor Chuwei because he was an advocate of living a free life. Known as a model for local officialdom, he had only been a small local official in the Song state and was called 'Proud Qi Yuan Lord'. He first presented the thoughts of 'sagacity within and kingliness without' which had a profound influence on Confucianism. Zhuang Zi's imagination was extremely rich. His speech was fluid and profound so that he could disseminate subtle and profound philosophical subjects in a nuanced manner. His representative works were collected in the famous *The Book of Articles* or *Zhuang Zi*, in which 'A Happy Excursion' and 'The Adjustment of Controversies' were the most famous parts. His works were referred as: 'the philosophy of literature or the literature of philosophy'. It is believed that Zhuang Zi lived in Nan Hua Mountain in seclusion, so he was called 'Nan Hua Zhenren' and his book, *Zhuang Zi*, was called Nan Hua's Scriptures.

庄子简介

庄子,战国中期思想家、哲学家和文学家。姓庄,名周,宋国蒙人,先祖是宋国君主宋戴公。他创立了华夏重要的哲学学派——庄学,是继老子之后,战国时期道家学派的代表人物。与老子并称为老庄。

庄子因崇尚自由而不应楚威王之聘,生平只做过宋国地方的漆园吏,史称"漆园傲吏"。被誉为地方官吏之楷模。庄子最早提出"内圣外王"思想对儒家影响深远,他的想象力极为丰富,语言运用自如,灵活多变,能把一些微妙难言的哲理说得引人入胜。代表作品为《庄子》,其中的名篇有《逍遥游》、《齐物论》等。其作品被人称之为"文学的哲学,哲学的文学"。据传,庄子又尝隐居南华山,故唐玄宗天宝初,被诏封为南华真人,称其著书《庄子》为《南华真经》。

Chapter Twenty-Seven

Lament One's Insignificance Before the Vast Ocean

WHEN AUTUMN CAME, IT RAINED heavily, and a lot of streams merged into the Yellow River. The waves were big, the river rose, and this flooded the sandbank and the shore. The surface of the river widened, and the cattle and horses could hardly be distinguished, especially from the other side of the river.

The sight was so spectacular that the observer Hebor thought that all of the water from the entire world had emerged there. He felt smug and walked along the river towards the east, watching the water.

Then he came to the North Sea and looked to the east. He was so surprised to see that the sky and water merged on the horizon. He did not know where the end of the water was.

Looking at the water for a while, he turned to the sea and said: 'As the saying goes, he who knows a little more than most, thinks himself to be the best and that he is the only person'.

Moral: not seeing any mountains, not manifesting the plains. Not seeing the sea, not knowing the streams. There are mountains outside of the mountains. There is the sky outside of the sky. Actually, everyone is relatively insignificant.

望洋兴叹

秋天来到,天降大雨,无数细小的水流,汇入黄河。只见波涛汹涌,河水暴涨,淹没了河心的沙洲,浸灌了岸边的洼地,河面陡然变宽,隔水远望,连河对岸牛马之类的大牲畜也分辨不清了。

眼前的景象多么壮观啊,河伯以为天下的水都汇集到他这里来了,不由洋洋得意。他随着流水向东走去,一边走一边观赏水景。

他来到北海,向东一望,不由大吃一惊,但见水天相连,不知道哪里是水的尽头。

河伯呆呆地看了一阵子,才转过脸来对着大海感慨地说:"俗话说:'道理懂得多一点的人,便以为自己比谁都强。'我就是这样的人啦!"

寓意:不见高山,不显平地;不见大海,不知溪流。山外有山,天外有天。我们每个人其实都是很渺小的。

Chapter Twenty-Eight

A Roc's Flight of Ten Thousand Miles

IN ANCIENT TIMES, THERE WAS a huge bird called a roc. Its back was as high as Mount Tai. When it flew, its wings were like clouds covering the sun.

One day, the roc flew to the South China Sea. Its wings hit the water and each span covered three thousand miles. Then it flew up in the sky, created a storm and flew ninety million miles. It took half a year each time to fly to the South China Sea and back. When it flew high, its back got close to the sky and the clouds were beneath it.

The little birds who lived in the low land, saw the roc flying so high and far away. They didn't understand this and asked: 'Where does it want to fly to? We fly a few feet or so and then fall, so when we fly around the sweet sage wort, we think that we have already reached the edge of the sky. Where on earth does the roc want to go to?'

Moral: it is hard for a short-sighted person to understand the pursuit of a high-minded one.

鹏程万里

远古的时候，有一种鸟，名字叫作鹏。大鹏鸟的背像泰山那样高，飞起来的时候，它的翅膀就像遮天蔽日的云彩。

有一次，大鹏鸟向南海飞去。它在南海海面上用翅膀击水而行，扇一下就是三千里。它向高空飞去，卷起一股暴风，一下子就飞出九万里。它飞出去一次，要过半年才飞回南海休息。当它飞向高空的时候，它的背靠着青天，而云层却在它的下边。

生活在洼地里的小安鸟雀，看见大鹏鸟飞得这么高，这么远，很不理解，就说："他还想飞到哪里去呢？我们往上飞，不过几丈高就落下来了，我们在蓬蒿飞来飞去，也算是飞到边了。大鹏鸟究竟想飞到什么地方去呢？"

寓意：一个目光短浅的人，是不能理解志向高远者的追求的。

Chapter Twenty-Nine

Marquis Lu Kept a Bird

ONCE UPON A TIME, A sea bird swooped down in the suburb of the capital of the Lu state. Marquis Lu thought it was a bird of God, so he ordered that it be caught. He personally sent the bird to the ancestral temple and greeted it respectfully with a feast.

They played the ancient music shaoyue for the bird every day and fed it with beef, lamb, and pork. The hospitality made the bird nervous and dizzy. It ate and drank nothing, not even water and so it died three days later. Marquis Lu raised the bird in his own way of providing pleasure but not according to the way of a bird. The bird was frightened to death by him.

Moral: the story is a metaphor for doing something according to one's own fancy but not to that of the subject. Like the Western idiom: 'The road to hell is paved with good intentions'. Work should be targeted, otherwise it is bound to fail.

鲁侯养鸟

从前，有只海鸟落在鲁国都城的郊外，鲁侯以为这是只神鸟，令人把它捉住，亲自把它迎接到祖庙里，毕恭毕敬地设宴迎接，并将它供养起来，每天都演奏古时的音乐《九韶》给它听，安排牛羊猪三牲具备的"太牢"给它吃。鲁侯的这种招待把海鸟搞得头晕目眩，惶恐不安，一点儿肉也不敢吃，一杯水也不敢喝，过了三天就死了。鲁侯是用他自己享乐的方式来养鸟的，而不是按照鸟的生活方式来养鸟啊。这只鸟是被他吓死的。

寓意：办事不看对象，完全根据自己的好恶行事，好心也会把事情办糟。

题旨：办事要有针对性，否则必然失败。

Chapter Thirty

Remove Bulls to Get Things Done

A COOK WAS CARVING UP an ox for the Emperor Liang Hui. Wherever his hand touched, his shoulder leaned, his foot trod, and his knee thrust. The sound of ripping and slicing was like a melodious rhythm that matched the music of Jingshou. His movements were like the dance of the Mulberry Grove and were rhythmic. The Emperor Liang Hui focused on this and was enchanted. He said: 'Ah! Very good! How did you achieve such a perfect skill?'

The cook put down his knife and replied: 'What I love is the Dao – this is more advanced than my skills. When I first began to carve up an ox, I saw nothing but the whole ox. I didn't know the inner structure of the ox and where to start.

'Three years later, I saw the crevices of the bones and veins instead of the whole ox. Now, I cutup the ox in my mind instead of my eyes, and I know how to operate. I follow the ox's natural veins, where my knife thrust is applied into the crevices between those muscles and joints. I never touch those bones, not even the big ones.

A good cook changes his knife every year when he uses it to cut. An ordinary cook changes it every month because he uses it to hack. My knife has been in use for nineteen years and has cut up thousands of oxen, and yet its edge is still as sharp as if it has just been whetted. Compared to the blade of the knife with crevices from those joints, it is much thinner. There is certainly plenty of space for the thin blade of the knife to work between those crevices. This is the reason why the blade of my knife that has been in use for nineteen years is still as sharp as a new one. Though I am skilful, I still proceed with caution. I fix my eyes on the object, moving slowly and cutting gently, so the part of the ox is quickly separated and then drops like mud sliding down to the ground. Then I can relax. I stand with the knife in my hand, looking around, cleaning the knife, and then put it away with satisfaction.'

Moral: all things in the world have their own laws, just absorb these and then everything can be handled smoothly. Let it go, follow its law, a stitch in time saves nine.

庖丁解牛

庖丁为梁惠王宰牛。手到的时候，肩倚的时候，脚踩的时候，膝顶的时候，那声音十分和谐，就跟美妙的音乐一样，合于尧时的《经首》旋律；那动作也很有节奏，就像优美的《桑林》舞蹈。梁惠王看得出了神，称赞说："哈，好啊！你的技术是怎么达到这样高超的地步的呢？"

庖丁放下刀对梁惠王说："我喜欢探求的是道，比一般的技术又进了一步。我开始解剖牛的时候，看到的无非是一头整牛，不知道牛身体的内部结构，不知道从什么地方下手。三年以后，我眼前出现的是牛的骨缝空隙，就不再是一头整牛。到了今天，我宰牛就全凭感觉了，不需要再用眼睛看来看去，就能知道刀应该怎么运作。牛的肌体组织结构都是有一定规律的，我进刀的地方都是肌肉和筋骨的缝隙，从不碰牛的骨头，更不消说碰大骨头了。

技术高明的厨师，一年换一把刀，因为他是用刀割。一般的厨师，一个月就更换一把刀，因为他是用刀砍。而我宰牛的这把刀，已经用了十九年；所宰的牛，又经有几千头，然而刀口锋利得仍然像刚在磨石上磨过的一样。这是为什么呢？就因为牛的肌体组织结构之间有空隙，而刀口与这些空隙比起来，薄得好像一点厚度也没有。用没有厚度的刀在有空隙的肌体组织间运行，当然绰绰有余！所以十九年过去，我的刀还跟新的一样。虽然我的技术已达到了这种程度，但我在解剖牛的时候，还是丝毫不敢马虎，总是小心翼翼，心神专注，进刀时不匆忙，用力时不过猛，牛体迎刃而解，牛肉就像一摊泥土一样从骨架上滑落到地上。这时，我才松下一口气来，提刀站立，顾视一下四周，心满意足地把刀揩拭干净，收藏起来。"梁惠王听了，高兴地说："好极了，听了你的这一席话，我从中悟到了修身养性的道理。"

寓意：世间一切事物，都有它自身的规律，掌握了事物的规律，办事就可以得心应手。

题旨：顺其自然，循其规律，事半功倍。

Chapter Thirty-One

Monkey Bravado

THE KING OF WU MEANDERED along the river in a boat, then climbed on a monkey mountain. All of the monkeys ran away in panic, hiding in thorns. Only one monkey jumped around triumphantly in front of the king, deliberately showing off its dexterity. The king took up a bow and shot at it, but the monkey quickly caught the arrow. The king ordered all of his soldiers to shoot at the monkey at once, and so it was killed. The king turned back to his friend Yan Buyi and said: 'The monkey boasted of his dexterity and was proud in front of me, so it died. Be cautious! Don't show off your position to others.' Upon returning home, Yan Buyi took sage Dong Wu as his teacher. He tried hard to overcome his pride and avoided beautiful women and other pleasures. He no longer appeared in public. Three years later, all the people in the country praised him.

Moral: no matter how capable you are, you shouldn't be proud of it. Be modest and cautious, and then you will be respected.

猴子逞能

吴王坐船在大江里游玩，攀登上一座猴山。一群猴子看见了，都惊慌地四散逃跑，躲在荆棘丛中了；唯独有一只猴子，却洋洋得意地跳来跳去，故意在吴王面前卖弄灵巧。吴王拿起弓箭向它射去，那猴子敏捷地把飞箭接住了。吴王下令左右的侍从一齐放箭，那只猴子被射死了。吴王回过头对他的朋友颜不疑说："这只猴子夸耀自己的灵巧，仗恃自己的敏捷，在我面前表示骄傲，以至于这样死去了。警惕呀！不要拿你的地位去向别人炫耀呀！"颜不疑回去以后，就拜贤人董梧为老师，尽力克服自己的骄气，远离美色声乐，不再抛头露面。过了三年，全国人都称誉他。

寓意：不管有多大的本领，也不可当作骄傲的本钱。谦虚谨慎，才能获得人们的敬重。

Chapter Thirty-Two

A Mere Copycat

XISHI WAS A VERY BEAUTIFUL girl. One time, she was suffering from heartache, so she maintained a cold heart and locked her eyebrows. An ugly girl saw this but still thought that Xishi looked very beautiful.

After she returned home, the ugly girl adopted this trait from Xishi. She also held a stone-hearted countenance and frowned, and thus sought praise for her beauty. When the rich men in the countryside saw her, however, they immediately closed the door. When the poor men saw her, they shuffled their wives and children far away from her. The ugly girl only knew the beauty of locking eyebrows but didn't know why that was beautiful.

Moral: if you do something without considering the practicalities but just blindly copy, it's easy to achieve the wrong result.

东施效颦

西施长得很美丽,即使是心口痛的时候,紧锁着双眉,附近的一个丑女见了,仍感到她的样子很漂亮.

丑女回去以后,也学着西施的样子,捧着心口,皱着眉头,想让别人夸她漂亮。谁知道乡里的富人看她这个样子,赶紧关闭大门不出来;穷人见了,也拉着自己的妻子儿女远远地躲开。这个丑女只知道皱着眉头的样子美,却不知道为什么皱眉的样子美。

寓意:做事情,如果不考虑自己的条件,盲目地模仿别人,很容易弄巧成拙,适得其反。

Chapter Thirty-Three

The Skill of Slaughtering a Dragon

THERE WAS A MAN WHOSE surname was Zhu. He intended to learn a kind of skill that nobody else had acquired before, so he went to achieve the ability to kill a dragon. He spent all of the family assets and three years later, he finally learned this unique skill.

Zhu returned home triumphantly but where was there a dragon in the world? As a result, he had learned a useless skill.

Moral: learning should be practical and realistic, and place emphasis on the actual achievement. If you break away from reality, no matter how capable you are, it is pointless.

屠龙之技

有一个姓朱的人，一心要学会一种别人都没有的技术，于是，就去学习宰杀龙的本领。他花尽了家里资产，用了整整三年时间，终于把宰杀龙的技术学到手了。

姓朱的得意洋洋地回到家里。可是，世间哪有龙可杀呢？结果，他学的技术一点也用不上。

寓意：学习必须从实际出发，讲求实效。如果脱离了实际，再大的本领也没有用。

Chapter Thirty-Four

Learning to Walk in Handan

DURING THE WARRING STATES PERIOD, there was a teenager in the Yan state, who heard that the walking gait of the Handan people in the Zhao state was considered very beautiful. He went to Handan to learn how to walk like them. As a result, he not only didn't succeed in accomplishing their walking gait, but also forgot his own. Finally, he had no option but to go home.

Moral: the one who completely denies his own tradition but just mechanically copies the experience of others, will not only lose himself, but won't be able to learn from others.

邯郸学步

燕国寿陵有个少年，千里迢迢来到邯郸，打算学习邯郸人走路的姿势。结果，他不但没有学到赵国人走路的样子，而且把自己原来走路的步子也忘记了，最后只好爬着回去。

寓意：全盘否定自己的传统，生搬硬套别人的经验。不仅学不到别人的优点，反而会丢掉自己的长处。

Chapter Thirty-Five

Using a Pearl to Shoot a Sparrow

THERE WAS A MAN WHO liked to hunt birds, using his pearl as a pellet to shoot any sparrow flying a thousand miles high in the sky. People who saw this laughed at him. This is because he paid a high price to achieve something insignificant.

Moral: when we do something, we should pay attention to its value. It is foolish to lose something valuable for a worthless thing.

随珠弹雀

有一个喜打鸟的人,却用随珠作弹丸,去射飞翔在千丈高空中的一只麻雀。人们看了都嘲笑他。这是什么道理呢?这是因为付出的代价太昂贵,而得到的东西太轻微。

寓意:做什么事,都得讲究得失轻重。为了没什么价值的东西而丢掉十分宝贵的东西,这是一种十分愚蠢的行为。

Chapter Thirty-Six

The Fight on The Horn of The Snail

DAI JINREN SAID TO THE Emperor Liang Hui: 'Do you know of a small animal called a snail?' The emperor replied: 'I do know'.

The Jin people said: 'There are two countries on the horn of the snail. One is called the Touching State and the other is called the Barbarian State. The two states often fight over territory. After each war, there are always corpses littered everywhere and tens of thousands of people die. It often takes more than ten days for the winning army to chase after the defeated one.'

The Emperor Hui said: 'Is this just your imagination?' The Jin people said: 'Allow us to prove it for you. Do you imagine that there is a boundary in an endless universe?' The emperor replied: 'No.'

The Jin people said: 'Free your imagination, and when you return to reality, you can only reach the earth. Isn't it insignificant compared to the reality of the imagination?' The emperor said: 'You are right.'

The Jin people said: 'There is the Wei state in the territory that we can reach. After the Wei state moved its capital to Liang, then there was the Liang state. Because there is the Liang state it follows that there is appearance of and the Emperor Liang. Is there therefore, any difference between the Emperor Liang and that of the barbarian?' The Emperor Hui thought about it and said: 'It seems that nothing is different.

After the Jin people left, the emperor was depressed and seemed to have lost something.

Moral: we are small in the world. We should cherish our lives and the world.

蜗角之争

戴晋人对梁惠王说:"您知道有一种名叫蜗牛的小动物吗?"梁惠王回答:"知道。"

晋人又说:"蜗牛的角上有两个国家,左角上的叫触国,右角上的叫蛮国。这两个国家经常为争夺地盘而发生战争。每次战争后,总是尸横遍野,死亡好几万人;取胜的国家追赶败军,常常要十多天才能回来。"惠王说:"呀!这都是您瞎编的吧!"晋人说:"请允许我来为您证明。您想象在广阔的宇宙中有边界吗?"

惠王说:"没有。"

晋人说:"您想象在宇宙中任意驰骋,而一回到现实中,您能够到达的地方却只限于四海九洲之内。拿现实的有限与想象的无穷相比,岂不是若有若无,微不足道吗?"

惠王说:"你说的对。"

晋人说:"在我们所能够到达的领域里有一个魏国,魏国迁都大梁后才有梁国,有梁国才有梁王。梁王与蛮氏,有什么不同吗?"

惠王想了想说:"好像没有什么不同。"

魏晋人走了以后,梁惠王情绪低落,好像丢失了什么。

寓意:在大千世界中,我们都是很渺小的。我们应该珍惜生命和让我们生存的这个世界,不应该为了蝇头小利或是一己之私利而破坏和平,从而付出极大的代价。

Chapter Thirty-Seven

Zhuang Zi is Fishing in the Pu River

ZHUANG ZI WAS FISHING IN the Pu River when the emperor of the Chu state sent two scholar-officials to invite him to become an official.

They said to Zhuang Zi: 'The problems of domestic affairs should rest on your shoulders!' Zhuang Zi took hold of a fishing rod and without looking at them, said: 'I heard that three thousand years ago there was a tortoise in the Chu state that had died. The emperor wrapped it with damask and honoured it in the hall of the temple. Would the tortoise rather die and leave its bones for people to cherish, or live in the mud and wag its tail?' The two scholar-officials said:'it would rather live and wag its tail in the mud.'

Zhuang Zi said: 'Please go back, I want to wag my tail in the mud.'

Moral: Zhuang Zi advocated spiritual freedom. He thought that all things in the universe are equal, and lives naturally have a spiritual power that is sufficient in itself. He rejected the opportunity to become a high official in the Chu state and stated that he would rather be like a tortoise living in the mud and waging its tail. He didn't want to be bound by a high position and despised the wealthy and powerful. This reflected his personality's independence, noble quality, and pursuit of the freedom of spirit.

庄子钓于濮水

庄子在濮河钓鱼，楚国国王派两位大夫前去请他（做官），（他们对庄子）说："楚王想劳烦您管理国内的政事呀！"庄子拿着鱼竿没有回头看（他们），说："我听说楚国有（一只）神龟，死了已有三千年了，国王用锦缎包好放在竹匣中珍藏在宗庙的堂上。这只（神）龟，（它是）宁愿死去留下骨头让人们珍藏呢，还是情愿活着在烂泥里摇尾巴呢？"

两个大夫说："情愿活着在烂泥里摇尾巴。"

庄子说："请回吧！我要在烂泥里摇尾巴。"

寓意：庄子是主张精神上的逍遥自在的，主张宇宙中的万事万物都具有平等的性质，生命自然流注出一种自足的精神的力量。他拒绝到楚国做高官，宁可像一只乌龟拖着尾巴在泥浆中活着，也不愿让高官厚禄束缚了自己。体现了他鄙弃富贵权势，不为官所累，坚持不受束缚，逍遥自在生活的高尚品质，表现了他对人格独立，精神自由的追求。

Chapter Thirty-Eight

A Medicine for Anti-Frostbite

HUIZI SAID TO ZHUANG ZI: 'The emperor of the Wei state sent me some cucurbit seeds. I planted them and now the fruit is growing so much that I need a volume of nearly five-stone dans (an ancient capacity unit in China). If it is used to hold water and drink, it is hard to lift up. If it is cut to make two ladles, it is too big to fit anything. It is not big enough, but it is useless, so I broke it.' Zhuang Zi said: 'You are really not adept at utilising such big things.'

There was a Song people who were good at producing a medicine to prevent frozen skin cracks. The ancestral generations had always washed cotton wool in water as a profession. Somebody heard about it and wanted to buy the prescription for a hundred gold (an ancient unit of measure in China). The whole family gathered together and discussed it: 'We've rinsed cotton wool for generations, but the revenue was only a little bit of gold. Now that we can gain a hundred pieces of gold by selling it, so please allow this to be done.' The man who bought the prescription did so to convince the emperor of the Wu state. At that time, the Yue state was invading the Wu state, so the emperor of the latter asked him to command the army and used the prescription as a medicine for them. In winter, they fought with the Yue army in a maritime war. As a result, the Yue army was defeated, so the emperor of Wu rewarded the man with a piece of land. The prescription is still the same one, but its usage is different. Now that you have a five-stone dans of cucurbits, why not consider floating it as a waist boat (an ancient buoy in China)? but just be worried ? Your heart is just like fluffy grass that is blocked.

Moral: if the same thing is used in a different way it may cause adverse effects. When dealing with things, we should actively explore the principle and be good at discovering and digging out the inner meaning so as to make best use.

不龟手之药

惠子对庄子说:"魏王送给我葫芦的种子,我把它种到成熟,结成的葫芦很大,有五石的容积。用来盛水和饮料,它的坚硬程度却禁不起举。剖开来作瓢,却因太大而没有适于它容纳的东西。不是它不够大,而是因为它没有用处,所以我把它打破了。"庄子说:"你实在是不善于利用大的东西。宋国有一个善于制作防止皮肤冻裂的药的人,祖祖辈辈以在水中漂洗棉絮为业。有人听说了,就请求用百金买他的药方。全家族的人集中在一起商议道:'我们世世代代漂洗棉絮,收入不超过几金。现在卖药方一下子可以得到百金,请允许我把药方卖给他。'那人得了药方,便用它去说服吴王。越国来侵犯吴国,吴王让他统帅军队。冬天和越军进行水战,把越军打得大败。吴王便将一块土地封赏给他。能不使手裂开的药是一样的,有的人靠它得到封赏,而有的人却免不了漂洗棉絮的辛劳,就是因为用途不同。现在你有五石容量的葫芦,为什么不考虑把它作为腰舟而浮游于江湖之上,反而担忧它大得无处可容,可见你的心如蓬草一样屈曲不通啊!"

寓意：同样的东西用在不同的地方，其效果大不一样。对待事物，要主动探究事理，善于发现，挖掘事物的内在价值，从而完美利用其最大价值。

Chapter Thirty-Nine

Zhuang Zi Dreaming That He Was a Butterfly.

ONE DAY, ZHUANG ZI DREAMT that he had become a butterfly and was flying with abandon between the flowers. He felt very happy and comfortable and totally forgot that he was Zhuang Zi. Suddenly he woke up, and he was surprised to discover that he was once again Zhuang Zi. So, he pondered whether he, Zhuang Zi, was dreaming that he was a butterfly or if he as a butterfly was dreaming that he was Zhuang Zi. There must be a difference between Zhuang Zi and the butterfly. This is called an integration and change of matter and oneself.

Moral: A butterfly is a symbol of freedom and beauty. Dreaming of being a butterfly, Zhuang Zi expressed his yearning for freedom. After waking up, he couldn't confirm whose dream it was – Zhuang Zi's or the butterfly's? He thought that reality and imagination sometimes were hard to distinguish. If people could see through the boundary between life and death, matter, and themselves, they would always be happy. He advocated a perspective of returning to a natural way, living with no burden, freely and happily.

庄周梦蝶

有一天,庄周梦见自己变成了蝴蝶,在花丛中自由自在的飞翔,感到十分快活和舒畅,已经完全忘记自己是庄周了。突然间醒过来,惊惶不定之间方知原来我是庄周。不知是庄周梦中变成蝴蝶呢,还是蝴蝶梦中变成庄周呢?庄周与蝴蝶那必定是有区别的。这就可叫作物、我的交合与变化。

寓意:蝴蝶是自由、美丽的象征,庄子通过对梦中变化为蝴蝶来表达对自由自在的向往。梦醒后蝴蝶复化为己的事件的进一步提出了人不可能确切的区分真实与虚幻和生死物化的观点。所谓"物化"是说:"要使人性复归,让人按照人原来的自然天性自由自在地、痛快淋漓地去生活。庄子认为人们如果能打破生死、物我的界限,则无往而不快乐。

Chapter Forty

Huizi Becoming the Prime Minister of The Liang State

HUIZI HAD BECOME THE PRIME minister of the Liang state. Zhuang Zi visited him. Somebody told Huizi: 'Zhuang Zi is coming and wants to replace you as the prime minister." Huizi therefore was very afraid of this happening, so he searched for three days and nights throughout the state for Zhuang Zi. Zhuang Zi went to see him and said: 'There is a bird in the south that is named the yuanchu, do you know it? The yuanchu flies from the South Sea to the North Sea. It only inhabits the sycamore tree, just eats the bamboo and only drinks from the sweet spring. One time, an owl picked up a rotten mouse while the yuanchu was flying nearby. The owl looked up and shouted angrily: "Do you want to scare me with the Liang state?"'

Moral: Zhuang Zi likened himself to yuanchu, Huizi to an owl, fortune, and fame to a rotten mouse. This expresses his stand of despising fortune and fame and satirised Huizi's paranoia. It advises us not to be suspicious when we don't know the truth or true intentions of others.

惠子相梁

惠施在梁国做宰相，庄子去看望他。有人告诉惠施说："庄子（到梁国）来，是想取代你做宰相。"于是惠施唯恐失去相位，在国都搜捕几天几夜。庄子前去见他，说："南方有一种鸟，它的名字叫鹓鶵，你知道它吗？那鹓鶵从南海起飞飞到北海去，不是梧桐树不栖息，不是竹子的果实不吃，不是甜美的泉水不喝。在此时猫头鹰拾到（一只）腐臭的老鼠，鹓鶵从它面前飞过，（鸱鹰）仰头看着，发出'喝！'的怒斥声。现在你也想用你的梁国（相位）来威胁我吗？"

寓意：这篇短文中，庄子将自己比作鹓鶵，将惠子比作猫头鹰，把功名利禄比作腐鼠，表明自己鄙弃功名利禄的立场和志趣，讽刺了惠子醉心于功名利禄且无端猜忌别人的丑态。

题旨：在还未了解别人的真实意图，或还未了解事情的真相时，切不可妄加猜忌。

Chapter Forty-One

Be Insensate like a Wooden Chicken

Ji Shengzi was raising a gamecock for Emperor Xuan. Ten days later, the emperor asked: 'Have you finished its training?'

Ji Shengzi said: 'Not yet, it is still proud and full of blood.'
Ten days later, the emperor asked again, Ji Shengzi said: 'Not yet, it is still staring fiercely at others.'

Another ten days passed, and the emperor repeated his question and Ji Shengzi answered: 'Almost done, when other gamecocks bark at it, it does not respond.'

The emperor went to check the gamecock and sure enough, it was like a wooden chicken. Its vigour, however, had inwardly transformed. No cock dared to fight with it, all of them quickly ran away immediately they saw it.

Moral: the phrase 'be insensate like a wooden chicken' was first used to describe a person's calm and stable attitude that is close to 'Still waters run deep'. Now it is used to describe a silly and frightened looking person.

呆若木鸡

纪渻子为宣王饲养斗鸡。十天后，宣王问道："鸡训练完毕了吗？"

纪渻子说："还不行，它正凭着一股血气而骄傲。"

过了十日，宣王又问训练好了没有。纪渻子说："还不行，仍然对别的鸡的啼叫和接近有所反应。"

再过十天，宣王又问，纪渻子说："还不行，仍然气势汹汹地看着（对方）。"

又过了十天，宣王又问。纪渻子说："差不多了，即使别的鸡叫，（斗鸡）已经没有任何反应了。"

宣王去看斗鸡的情况，果然就像木头鸡了，可是它的精神全凝聚在内，别的鸡没有敢应战的，看见它转身逃走了。

寓意：呆若木鸡"最早是形容一个人镇静自若，态度稳重，和"大智若愚"比较贴近。现在成语呆若木鸡就只剩字面意思了，用来形容一个人有些痴傻发愣的样子，或因恐惧或惊异而发愣的样子。

Chapter Forty-Two

Liezi Archery

LIE YUKOU WAS DEMONSTRATING HIS archery for Bohun Wuren. He stretched his bowstring and put a cup of water on his elbow, then he dispatched the first arrow. Just before it reached the target, he immediately shot the second one. Then he shot the third one, before the second one had landed. At that moment, Lie Yukou just looked like a puppet without any movement. Bohun Wuren saw this and said: 'This is just a predetermined performance but not spontaneous archery. I want to climb the mountain with you and see if, whilst walking along the edge of a dangerous cliff and looking down into the abyss, you can still shoot an arrow'.

So, they went to the cliff and whilst staring into the abyss, and with a part of his feet suspended in the air, he let Lie Yukou shoot. His companion, Liezi was so frightened that his sweat ran straight down to his heels. Bohun Wuren said: 'A superior self-cultivated master can observe the sky and yet dares to go the netherworld. His spirit freely reaches throughout the universe, but his face will never change. You are so frightened now, so it is too difficult for you to shoot the target.'

Moral: The archer should not be affected by the external environment. He must keep to the Dao and forget everything outside, then can he reach the utmost of perfection.

列子射箭

　　列御寇为伯昏无人表演射箭的本领，他拉满弓弦，又放置一杯水在手肘上，发出第一支箭，箭还未至靶的紧接着又搭上了一支箭，刚射出第二支箭而另一支又搭上了弓弦。在这个时候，列御寇的神情真像是一动也不动的木偶人似的。伯昏无人看后说："这只是有心射箭的箭法，还不是无心射箭的射法。我想跟你登上高山，脚踏危石，面对百丈的深渊，那时你还能射箭吗？"

　　于是伯昏无人便登上高山，脚踏危石，身临百丈深渊，然后再背转身来慢慢往悬崖退步，直到部分脚掌悬空这才拱手恭请列御寇跟上来射箭。列御寇伏在地上，吓得汗水直流到脚后跟。伯昏无人说："一个修养高尚的'至人'，上能窥测青天，下能潜入黄泉，精神自由奔放达于宇宙八方，神情始终不会改变。如今你胆战心惊有了眼花恐惧的念头，你要射中靶的不就很困难了吗？"

　　提示：射箭绝不能受外界环境的影响，必须内守大道，外忘一切，才能达到出神入化的妙境。

Chapter Forty-Three

Debating about the Fish with Hui Shi

ZHUANG ZI AND HUI SHI WERE looking at some fish. Zhuang Zi said: 'The fish are swimming around so happily! Hui Shi was an expert in logical debate, so replied: 'You aren't a fish, how do you know if the fish are happy or not?" Zhuang Zi smiled and answered with the same logic: 'You aren't me, so how do you know that I don't know if the fish are happy or not?'

Moral : this is a famous debate using logic. Somebody said it was choplogic. Actually, Zhuang Zi was telling Hui Shi not to impose his theory on others, because he couldn't supplant theirs.

与惠施论鱼

庄子与惠施在濠上观鱼。庄子说："鱼游来游去，多么快乐呵"惠施是逻辑论辩的专家，马上抓住一点："你不是鱼，你怎么知道鱼的快乐呢？"庄子一笑，以同样的逻辑回答："你也不是我，你怎么知道我不懂鱼的快乐呢？"

寓意：在逻辑学上，这是著名的一例。有人说在逻辑上庄子有些诡辩。但实际上这说的是另一回事：庄子告诉惠施，不要把你的学说强加于人，因为你不能代替别人。

Chapter Forty-Four

Fear of the Shadow

A man was afraid of his own shadow. The more quickly he ran, the more the increase in his footprints and the narrower became his shadow that followed him. He thought that he still ran too slowly, so he ran harder and harder and at last exhausted himself until he died.

The man didn't know how to stop in the dark, so there would be no shadow; to be static so there would be no footprints. Sadness! What a foolish man he was!

Moral: in the final analysis, the man who is neurotic and suspicious will always harm himself.

畏影恶迹

一个人害怕自己的影子,讨厌自己的脚印,想摆脱它们,便快步跑起来。可是跑得越快,脚印越多;影子追得越紧。他自己认为还跑得太慢,更加拼命地跑下去,最后精疲力竭累死了。

这个人不知道在阴暗的地停下来,就不会有影子;静止不动,就不会有脚印,可悲呀,真是太愚蠢了!

题旨:神经过敏、疑神疑鬼、自遭其害。

Chapter Forty-Five

Zhuang Zi Borrows Some Rice

Zhuang Zi was very poor. When he didn't have any rice for cooking, he went to borrow some from a low official with whom he had made acquaintance. The official was mean, stingy but also wily. He knew he couldn't refuse him, so he said: 'Well, when I return with the rent from the city, I will lend you three hundred pieces of gold. Okay?'

Zhuang Zi's disposition quickly changed to that of anger: 'When I came here yesterday, suddenly I heard a voice of "help" in the hallway. A fish said to me: "I am the courier of the Dragon King of the Easter Sea. Unfortunately, I fell down here, could you please help me with a bucket of water to save my life?" I said: "Well. I am going to the south to lobby the kings of the Wu and Yue states, so the water of the Xi River will be brought to you here and so you will be saved. Okay?"

'The fish heard that and angrily changed his disposition and said: "I am already losing my life force and cannot survive. Only a bucketful of water can now save my life, however, you tell me this nonsense. It will be too late to wait for you to bring water from the Wu and Yue states. You would be better off soon looking for me at the salted fish shop."

Moral: an empty promise may kill people.

庄子借粮 涸辙之鲋

庄子很穷，没米下锅时，记得监河侯的小官和自己有一面之交，就向他借米。监河侯是个小气鬼，但也是个诡计多端的人。他推辞不掉，就说："好呵，等此时候吧，我把封邑的租子收回来了，可以给你价值三百余的粮米，让你吃个痛快。"

庄子悠然坐下："我刚才在路上听到一阵呼救的声音，找了半天，原来是一条小鲫鱼。它被什么人扔在车轮辗出的泥糟子里，它对我说它快要渴死了，先拿点水给它活命。我想呢，一点水只能救得一时，就答应它到南方游说吴越，让他们兴修水利，造一条渠把水引到这里来，你说我这个办法如何？"

监河侯也趣："那样还不如到干鱼滩上找它呢。好吧，我先拿点给你。"

题旨：空头支票害死人。

Chapter Forty-Six

Exceeding One's Duty and Meddling in Others' Affairs

EMPEROR RAO WANTED TO BEQUEATH the throne to Xu You, but he refused to accept it and said: "You have been the emperor for many years and have efficiently managed the state and yet you have nominated me to take your place. Should I lead the world just for the fame? So-called reputation is just empty, and I therefore do not wish to pursue it. You see, the wren nesting uses just a few branches from the forest. The rat can consume only as much water as its stomach will allow. The world to me is useless, so please forget it. Even if the cook doesn't produce any food for the sacrifice, the priest still can't replace him as cook.'

The Chinese sacrifice often entails first offering some dishes to the ancestors before the food can be eaten. So, the cook will first make the dishes and then the priest can ask the ancestors for blessings.

Moral: trust is very important and doesn't replace others' position and work.

越俎代庖

唐尧（想）把天下让给许由，说："日月出来了，然而仍然不熄灭小火把，它和日月比起，不也是没有意义了吗？及时雨降了，然而仍然灌溉，它对于润泽不也是徒劳吗？先生存在，天下被治理，然而我仍然掌控它，我自己认为我不足，请（允许我）让出天下。"

许由说："您治理天下，已经很好。然而我仍然代替你，我带领天下难道为了名声吗？名声，是'已经治理天下'这个事实的附属品？我带领天下是为了附属品吗？鹪鹩在森林筑巢，不过占一棵树枝；鼹鼠喝黄河里的水，不过喝饱自己肚皮。天下对我有什么用呢？你回去吧，算了吧，给我天下没有有用的地方啊！厨师即使不做祭祀用的饭菜，管祭祀人也不能越位来代替他下厨房做菜。"

题旨：充分相信群众，不要包办代替。

Chapter Forty-Seven

Tengyuan's Speciality

'YOUR MAJESTY, HAVE YOU SEEN an animal called the tengyuan?

They live in the tall, dense nanmu, catalpa and camphorwood areas. They cling on to the tall stems and dense branches. They come and go in their midst – up and down, acting as though they are the overlords of the forest. Even the great archers like Hou Yi and Peng Meng cannot easily shoot them. Once they fall down into the thorns and bushes, however, they become lethargic and indecisive. They will panic and become very afraid. It is not because their bodies have become inflexible but because of the hostile environment. In this condition, they cannot give full play to their climbing abilities.'

Moral: Only if there is an opportunity to display one's talents, can one put to good use one's potential.

腾猿处势

庄子穿着打有补钉的麻制粗布衣服，用麻绳细致整齐地系好鞋子，前往拜访魏王。魏王见了说："先生的处境为什么如此困病潦倒呢？"庄子说："是贫穷，不是困病潦倒。读书人身怀道德而不能用，这才叫困病潦倒；衣服破旧，鞋子穿孔，这是贫穷，而不是困病潦倒。这就是所谓没有遇到好时势，人们叫做'生不逢时'。大王难道没见过那腾跃自如的猿猴吗？它们生活在楠木、梓树、异木豫章那样的古木参天的森林里，攀缘腾跃树枝之间而称王为首，即使是神箭手羿和逢蒙也不敢小看它们。当它们到达桑树、荆棘、拐枣那样矮小的灌木丛中，就会小心翼翼地行动，而且不时地左顾右盼，内心震颤惊恐得周身发抖。这并不是因为它们筋骨紧缩而不再柔软灵活，而是所处的环境很不利，不但不足以充分施展身手，而且还会引起麻烦。"

题旨：有用武之地，英雄人物方可施展才能。

Chapter Forty-Eight

The Contented Louse Being a Parasite on Pigs

There are some lice that are parasitic to pigs. They move among those rough bristles, thinking that they occupy the imperial court and gardens. They feel cheerful and confident. They crowd in the hidden crotch, hoofs and breasts and think that they live in a quiet and rich paradise.

They don't know however, that when the butcher arrives, they will kill the pig and fire up those bristles. Then they will die, together with the pig.

Moral: living just for the sake of remaining alive while being self-absorbed will, in the final analysis, lead to a sad fate.

豕虱濡需

有种苟且偷安的东西，就是寄生在猪身上的那些虱子。它们选择在粗疏的毛鬃之间回旋，自以为占据的是帝王宽广的宫廷和园林，洋洋自得；拥挤在股胯蹄脚和乳房之间曲深隐蔽的地方，还以为得天独厚地生活在宁静富饶的乐园而欢天喜地。

它们却不知，一旦屠夫到来，动手屠宰，点火燎毛，自己将和猪一起同归于尽。

题旨：苟且偷生，自我陶醉，命运可悲。

Chapter Forty-Nine

The Dress and Food of the Sacrificial Calf

HAVE YOU EVER SEEN THE calf ready for sacrifice? It is dressed in a silk-embroidered colourful blanket and eats grass and beans mixed with fine feed and seems to be unique and superior. When it is dragged to the temple to get ready for the butchering, it is impossible for it to go back to the cattle pen to be an ordinary calf again.

Moral: do not be caught in the trap, or you will be deceived, and it will be too late for regret.

牺牛衣食

您见过供祭礼使用的牛吗?您看它,身披丝绣的五彩花巾,吃着草、豆拌成的上等饲料,似乎得天独厚,超群一等。待到被牵入太庙屠宰,再想获得自由,回到圈里做一头普通的犊牛,也不可能了。

题旨:勿入圈套,否则上当受骗,后悔不及。

Chapter Fifty

Forgetting Safety for Profit

ONE DAY, ZHUANG ZI WAS playing in a garden. He saw a strange bird flying in from the south. The bird was seven chi (an ancient measure unit in China) and flew past Zhuang Zi. It even touched his forehead, but it was oblivious to the fact and finally fell down in the chestnut woods.

Zhuang Zi felt that this was odd and said: 'What sort of bird is this? Its wings are so big, but it cannot fly far, its eyes are so big, but it cannot see clearly.'

Zhuang Zi lifted his robes and went forward, holding a slingshot in his hand, looking for an opportunity to hit it.

At this time, he saw a cicada hiding leisurely in the shade, totally oblivious to any danger. Beside it, a mantis hid under a leaf and eagerly prepared itself to catch the cicada. The bird was so intent on hunting the mantis that it had lost its attention.

Moral: don't forget danger when anticipating profit or you will put yourself in danger; be prepared for danger in times of safety and you will be on the safe side.

见利忘危

一天,庄周在雕陵栗园游玩,看见一只奇异的鹊鸟自南方飞来。这只鹊鸟翼长七尺,目大径寸,从庄周面前飞过,触到他的额头,也不理会,最后落在栗树林中。

庄周奇怪地说:"这是什么鸟啊,翅膀如此大,却飞不远;眼睛这样大,却看不清?"

于是撩起衣裳,起步走上前去,手拿弹弓,寻找机会弹射它。

这时,又看见一只知了,躲在浓荫,悠然自得地乘凉,忘记了自身的安危;旁边,一只螳螂隐藏在一枝树叶后面,蠢蠢欲动,得意忘形,准备捕食知了;那只奇异的鹊鸟一心想猎取螳螂,以致利令智昏,忘乎所以。

题旨:见利忘危,则危在旦夕;居安思危,则有备无患。

Chapter Fifty-One

True Morality Isn't Boasting

ON HIS WAY TO THE Song state one evening, Bole went into a hotel. He saw two of the owner's concubines: one was beautiful and the other ugly. However, the ugly one's position was high while that of the beautiful one was low. Bole was surprised and asked the owner about this. He said: 'The beautiful girl thinks herself beautiful, but I don't appreciate her simple, apparent beauty. The ugly girl is self-aware, and she has spiritual beauty, so I don't think she is ugly.'

After hearing this, Bole told his students with feeling: 'Keep this in mind! A noble man will not show off his virtuous character, wherever he goes, so he will be admired and appreciated by people."

贤不自贤

伯乐去宋国的途中，晚上到旅馆住宿。看见旅馆的青年店主有两个小妾，一个貌美，一个貌丑。那个貌丑的地位高，貌美的地位低。伯乐感到奇怪，问那店主是什么缘故。店主人说："貌美的自以为美，但我并不赏识她单纯的外在美；貌丑的却有自知之明，有了这样的心灵美，所以我并不觉得她丑。"

听了这番话，伯乐深有感触地告诉弟子们说："弟子们要牢记啊！一个行为高尚的人，却不炫耀自己贤良的品行，那么他无论走到哪里，怎能不格外受人敬重和爱戴呢！"

Chapter Fifty-Two

A Frog Living in a Well

A FROG LIVING IN A well boasted to a giant turtle from the East China Sea: 'How happy I am. I jumped out of the well and climbed on to the fence and skipped and played as much as I could. When I became tired, I went back to the well and hid in the hole, resting comfortably.

I jumped into the water, just being immersed up to my armpit and gently rested my chin. The mud just passed my feet, soft and comfortable. Look around, those shrimps, crabs, and tadpoles, no one is as happy as I. I monopolise the well and enjoy myself, this is fantastic. Why not come in and have a look?'

The turtle accepted the frog's invitation and was about to enter the well to take a look when its right leg was caught in the rail as it was about to step in with its left, so it slowly retreated and stood beside it.

The turtle told the frog about the wonders of the sea. How big it was, even using the measure of thousands of miles would be insufficient to describe its vastness. Using a mountain as a measure would not be enough to describe its depth.

During the time of Xia Yu, it rained heavily for nine out of ten years and there was flooding, yet the sea's surface did not increase at all. During the Shantang period, there was severe drought for eight years and yet the coast did not decrease one bit.

井底之蛙

住在浅井中的一只青蛙对来自东海的巨鳖夸耀说:"我生活在这里真快乐呀!高兴时,就跳到井外面,攀援到栏干上,尽情地蹦跳玩耍。玩累了,就回到井中,躲在井壁的窟窿里,舒舒服服地休息休息。跳进水里时,井水仅仅浸没我的两腋,轻轻地托住下巴;稀泥刚刚没过双脚,软软的很舒适。看看周围的那些小虾呀、螃蟹呀、蝌蚪呀,谁也没有我快乐。而且我独占一井水,尽情地享受其中的乐趣,这样的生活真是美极了。您为什么不进来看一看吧!"

巨鳖接受了井蛙的邀请,准备到井里去看看,但它的左脚还没有跨进去,右腿已被井的栏干绊住了,只好慢慢地退回去,站在井旁边给青蛙讲述海的奇观:"海有多大呢?即使用千里之遥的距离来形容也表达不了它的壮阔,用千丈之高的大山来比喻,也比不上它的深度。夏禹的时候,十年有九年下大雨,大水泛滥成灾,海面不见丝毫增高;商汤的时候,八年有七年天大旱,土地都裂了缝,海岸也丝毫不见降低。不因时间的长短而改变,也不因雨量的多少而增减,生活在东海,那才真正是快乐呢!"

井蛙听了，吃惊得好半天也没有说出话来。它这才知道自己生活的地方是多么渺小。

寓意：人如果长期把自己束缚在一个狭小的天地里，就会变得目光短浅，自满自足。

题旨：盲目自满，自我陶醉，必授人以笑柄。

Chapter Fifty-Three

The Utility of Usefulness

HUIZI TOLD ZHUANG ZI: 'I have a big tree that people call useless. Its trunk is lumpy, so even a skilful carpenter can't draw a straight line on it with ink. Its twigs are so tangled that neither a compass nor an angle rule can be used. It grows just beside the road but the carpenters passing by ignore it. Just like your doctrines, most of which are useless, so most people abandon them.'

Zhuang Zi said: 'Have you ever seen a bobcat? It bows its body, hiding in the dark, quietly waiting for small animals. This is its special hunting ability. However, when it becomes highly conceited, it jumps east and west, up, and down, so it is inevitable that it falls prey to a hunter and finally perishes in the net. A yak has a huge body that is formidable, but it can't catch a mouse.

Now you have a big tree, but you dislike its uselessness. Why not plant it somewhere where nothing grows, or in a boundless suburb. You can wander leisurely under it or lie beside its shadow, so even a useless tree won't be cut by an axe or be damaged. A big tree may be useless, but it can avoid disaster and pain.

无用之用

惠子告诉庄子说:"我有一颗大树,人们称之为无用之材。粗大的主干疙疙瘩瘩,即便是手艺高超的木工工匠,也无法用墨绳画线取直;树的小枝卷曲,也不能用圆规和角尺量材取用。它虽然生长在大路旁边,可是路过的工匠却不屑一顾。这就像你的学说一样,大而无用,许多人都纷纷抛弃它啊!"

庄子说:"您难道没看见那山猫的样子吗?它低下身子潜藏暗处,静候那些出洞嬉戏的小动物,这是它捕食的特殊本领。但它得意忘形不守本分的时候,却东跳西窜,不避高低。所以最终免不了落入捕捉鸟兽的机关,死于山脊上的罗网。还有那牦牛,庞大的身躯就像挂在天边的云团,此物的本事数得上很大了,可是它却不能捉到老鼠。

如今您有大树,却又嫌弃大树无用。何不将它栽种到什么也不生长的地方,或者辽阔空旷无边无际的郊外。您就可以无所事事地悠游于树旁,逍遥自在地躺卧在树下。这样,无用的大树,就不会夭折于伐木的刀斧之下,也没有什么东西会去伤害它。大树虽然无处可用,哪里还会备受人间的苦痛与灾难呢?"

Chapter Fifty-Four

God Will Sometimes Miscalculate

IN THE MIDDLE OF THE night, the emperor of the Song state dreamt that a dishevelled man peeped from behind the door. He said to him: 'I come from a deep pool, and when I set off to the manor of the River God, a fisherman called Yu Qie caught me.'

The emperor woke up and called for someone to divine. The diviner said: 'It is a divine tortoise.' The emperor asked his servant: 'Is there a fisherman called Yu Qian?' The servant answered: 'Yes.' Yu Qian was brought in to meet the emperor the next day.

He had definitely caught a white tortoise that was five chi long (an ancient measure unit in China). The emperor asked him to divine the tortoise. The emperor had thought to kill it, but instead he hesitated and wondered whether to feed it, until the diviner said: 'If the divine tortoise is killed and its shell is used for division, it will be accurate.' Thus, it was killed and gutted. It was used for divination and there was never a miscalculation.

Zhuang Zi said: 'The tortoise could appear in the emperor's dream, but it wasn't able escape from the fisherman's net. It had the divine ability and none of its divination ever failed but it couldn't avoid the disaster of being gutted. Therefore, even though possessing a superior intelligence, one will still land in hot water. Even God may be thoughtless sometimes. Though he has mastered extraordinary wisdom, it will still be difficult to deal with ambushes from all sides. A free fish may not be afraid of the fisherman's net, but it will still be afraid of the huge mouth of a pelican.'

Abandoning tricks can really show great wisdom, removing the intent of good deeds can return one back to a natural character. An infant can speak without teaching if he gets along with people naturally.

Moral: The divine tortoise wanted to get rid of killing so it appeared in the dream of the emperor. Unfortunately, it was still killed, and its shell was used for divination. If it hadn't appeared in the dream, it might not have end up so miserably.

神有不及

宋元君半夜里，梦见有人披头散发在大厅侧门窥视，说："我来自清江江畔一个叫宰路的深潭，因为出使河神的领地，渔夫余且捉到了我。"宋元君醒来，叫人占卜，占卜的人说："那是一只神龟。"宋元君问："有名叫余且的渔夫吗？"侍臣回答说："有。"宋元君说："命令余且来见我。"第二天，余且到达朝廷之上。宋元君问："你捕到什么了？"余且回答说："我网到一只大白龟，周长五尺。"宋元君说："把白龟献上来。"余且送上白龟，宋元君两次三番想杀掉，又想喂养起来，正在犯难，占卜的人说："杀掉白龟用来占卜，一定大吉。"于是杀掉白龟挖空腹腔，用这只神龟的龟板占卜，七十二次推究事理，没有一次失算。

孔子说："神龟能托梦给宋元君，却不能躲过余且的鱼网；有神术智能，占卜数十次没有失误，却不能逃脱剖腹挖肠的灭顶之灾。如此说来，即便才智过人也会遭人陷阻围困，神灵也有考虑不周的地方。虽然有通天的智慧，也会遭到万人的谋算而难以应对。鱼儿即使不畏惧鱼网却也会害怕鹈鹕。摒弃小聪明方才显示大智慧，除去矫饰的善行方才能使自己真正回到自然的善性。婴儿生下地来没有高明的老师指教也能学会说话，只因为跟会说话的人自然相处。

题旨：神龟想免去杀身之祸，托梦给宋元君，没想到仍不免被剖杀，还被宋元君用其龟甲占卜，神龟若不托梦，下场也许还不至于这么惨.

Chapter Fifty-Five

Forgetting the Feet Because of a Pair of Comfortable Shoes

IT IS SAID THAT THERE was a skilful man around called Chui, during the Emperor Yao's lifetime. He could produce all kinds of illustrations that were even better than if he had used a graphic tool. His deft hands seemed to have the help of gods and ghosts so he could draw everything without calculation. He was just like a creator of nature. His work was so fantastic just because his mind was as free as a pool of clean water and unfettered.

Harmonising his spirit and the external environment, there is nothing that can embarrass you. Forgetting your feet is because your shoes are comfortable; forgetting your waist is because your belt is comfortable; forgetting right and wrong, that's because your heart is comfortable. It is appropriate to do things without easily changing your mind and to not follow the secular trends. The advantage of forgetfulness of one's mind is to let nature take its course. This is the natural law.

忘足适屦

相传尧帝时，有一个主理百工的巧匠，名字叫倕，他能很快地随手画出各式各样的图形，胜过校正圆形和方形的工具。灵巧的双手有如鬼神助之，他以手指随着物形的变化而变化，根本不用计算考虑，简直就像一个自然界的创造者。之所以这样，原因是他的心灵一清如水而不受约束。

解除外部环境与精神的束缚，就没有什么东西可以困扰你了。忘记了脚，是因为鞋舒服；忘记了腰，是因为腰带舒服；忘记了是非，是因为心里舒服；在内不轻易改变心志，在外不随从世俗潮流，是处事之合适。忘掉合适之合适，即顺其自然的安适，也就是符合自然法则之合适。

Chapter Fifty-Six

Divine Workmanship

Using his knives, Ziqing carved wood into beast-shaped pillars of bells and drums. After finishing, everyone was surprised about his divine workmanship. The Marquis Lu saw this and asked: 'How are you able to do that?'

Ziqing answered: 'I am just a worker, what skills could I have? I don't have any special skills, but there is one aspect to me that is different to that of others. When I begin to make a beast-shaped pillar, I will not distract my spirit and will fast with a faithful heart.

'After fasting for three days, I won't have any idea of granting a reward, conferring titles, and receiving salaries. After fasting for five days, I won't care about others' criticism. After fasting for seven days, I will be completely calm and even forget my own body. When this moment comes, there is no consideration for public and private or for the court, so my attention is focused.

'Then I will go to the forest, observing the attributes of all kinds of wood, selecting the best appearance and value of each, and thereby a divine and unique idea bursts forth. Under these circumstances, I begin to do my job, otherwise, I will stop. The reason for my divine workmanship is the combination of my pure character with the nature of the wood as one.'

Moral: Zhuang Zi thought that only if he reaches this state, can he create divine works. Eliminating interference from the outside and keeping a calm spirit within, watching the sky with a faithful heart, combining it with nature, this is the superior way of human behaviour. This is a metaphor for harmony between humans and Heaven.

鬼斧神工

梓庆能削刻木头做鐻，鐻做成以后，看见的人无不惊叹好像是鬼神的工夫。鲁侯见到便问他，说："你用什么办法做成的呢？"

梓庆回答道："我是个做工的人，会有什么特别高明的技术！虽说如此，我还是有一种本事。我准备做鐻时，从不敢随便耗费精神，必定斋戒来静养心思。斋戒三天，不再怀有庆贺、赏赐、获取爵位和俸禄的思想；斋戒五天，不再心存非议、夸誉、技巧或笨拙的杂念；斋戒七天，已不为外物所动仿佛忘掉了自己的四肢和形体。正当这个时候，我的眼里已不存在公室和朝廷，智巧专一而外界的扰乱全都消失。然后我便进入山林，观察各种木料的质地；选择好外形与体态最与鐻相合的，这时已形成的鐻的形象便呈现于我的眼前，然后动手加工制作；不是这样我就停止不做。这就是用我木工的纯真本性融合木料的自然天性，制成的器物疑为神鬼工夫的原因，恐怕也就出于这一点吧！"

题旨：庄子认为创作者只有达到这种境界，才能创作出与自然相合、与天工同化的出神入化的作品。本文提出了"心斋"的概念，就是心灵没有任何外界的干扰和杂念，进入"无待"的境界。梓庆依三个步骤依次淡忘了利、名、我，才能以我的自然和木的自然相应合，以天观天，以天合天，做出了鬼斧神工的钟架。这也是人们行为的最高境界。这则小品写一位专技者梓庆的精修用心的过程，以喻与自然为一的道理。

题旨：庄子认为创作者只有达到这种境界，才能创作出与自然相合、与天工同化的出神入化的作品。心灵没有任何外界的干扰和杂念，以天观天，以天合天，这也是人们行为的最高境界，以喻与自然为一的道理。

Chapter Fifty-Seven

Digging Apertures for Hundun

THE KING OF THE SOUTH China Sea was called Shu. The king of the North China Sea was called Hu. The king in the middle was called Hundun. Shu and Hu moved fast, and they usually gathered at Hundun's palace.

Hundun was natural, honest, and always treated them with hospitality, so Shu and Hu wanted to pay him back. They stated : 'Everybody has eyes, ears, nostrils, and mouth, only Hundun doesn't have them, so his face is obscure with nothing on it. Why not dig the seven apertures for him and allow him to taste food, listen to music, view scenery, and breathe fresh air? That would be good!'

Shu and Hu were aiming for the moon and opinionatedly believed this to be correct. One day, they produced an aperture for Hundun but what made things worse was that he unfortunately died.

Moral: everything has its attributes, if you try to superimpose on these, it will be counterproductive.

浑沌开窍

南海的大帝名叫倏，北海的大帝名叫忽，中央的大帝叫浑沌。来去匆匆的倏与忽过从甚密，他们常常相约到浑沌的住地聚会。自然淳朴的浑沌，总是非常友好地款待他们。

倏和忽发自内心的感激，便在一起商量，怎样才能报答浑沌的深厚情义，他们说："人人都有两眼、两耳、两鼻孔和嘴七个有孔的重要器官，唯独浑沌的面貌模糊一团，什么都没有。我们何不试着为他凿出七窍，也让他能跟我们一样，天天品尝美食佳肴、感受音乐的情趣、观赏人间的美景，呼吸清新的空气，那该多好啊！"

倏和忽凭自己想入非非，自以为是，给浑沌每天凿出一孔，结果却弄巧成拙，凿了七天，浑沌就死了。

题旨：事物皆有其特殊性，强求一律，反而坏事。

Chapter Fifty-Eight

A One-legged Beast and a Millipede

ONE DAY, A ONE-LEGGED beast was walking along the road, bouncing up and down with unbridled joy. A millipede passed by, and the one-legged beast couldn't help staring at it and said: 'Hi, my millipede friend, I think that jumping with one leg is very easy. Now you are walking with ten thousand feet, how do they work?'

The millipede proudly answered: 'I just walk like this, but I don't know how.' Then it walked away and saw a snake slithering in the long grass along the road. The millipede was surprised and asked the snake: 'Gosh! I walk with many feet, but I am still not as fast as you, why?' The snake calmly answered: 'I was born to move like this, I walk fast but I don't need any feet.'

One day, the snake met with the wind. 'Hello, wind, how free you are, and your speed is so remarkable.' The snake thought like a philosopher and so replied : 'I move using my waist and back and they are just like feet. You howled from the North Sea to the South Sea and left no songs. You are invisible but faster than me. How could you do this? Does the wind envy anything?'

'Yes,' the wind said: 'I envy eyes.'

What about eyes? Do eyes envy anything?

Eyes envy the heart.

The one-legged beast, the millipede, the snake, the wind......When did these conversations take place? It may have been a long time ago. Anyway, Zhuang Zi recorded these dialogues. The fable actually points to our hearts. We always envy others but don't cherish what we have already have. This results in losing ourselves. Don't envy others so your hearts may become calm. Everything has its existing value, and everybody has their uniqueness. There is no need to envy others.

独脚兽与多足虫

独脚兽走在路上，它蹦蹦跳跳，无拘无束，觉得自己快活又自由。

一条长长的多足虫在一边走过，独脚兽看着看着，忍不住有点发了呆。

"嗨，多足虫，我觉得自己用一条腿蹦跳，再也没有谁比我走路更简单。现在你用一万只脚走路，你是怎么走法呀？"

"反正我就这样走，我自己也不知道怎么会这样。"多足虫骄傲的说。

多足虫走啊走，路边的草丛里游过一条蛇。

多足虫很惊讶："哎呀，我用好多脚走路，却不如你走得快，蛇，这是为什么？"

蛇淡淡的说："我天生就是这样走，我走得快，哪里需要什么脚呀？"

蛇又遇见了风。

"风，你是多么自由，你的速度是多么让人羡慕，"蛇像一个哲学家那样思考着说，"我靠腰和脊背行走，还是像有脚一样的。你呼啸着从北海那儿刮过来,又呼啸着吹入南海,却像是没有形迹。你无形,却比我更快,怎么会这样?"

风是否也羡慕谁呢?

"是的,"风说,"我羡慕眼睛。"

眼睛呢,它又羡慕什么?

眼睛羡慕的,是人的心灵。

独角兽、多足虫、蛇、风……它们的对话到底发生哪一天?那是很久很久了吧,反正,两千多年前有位名叫庄周的人,已经记录过那天发生的事。庄子的寓言故事实际是我们内心的写照,我们总在羡慕别人,却不知道珍惜自己所有,羡慕别人的代价,常常就是失去自己。不去羡慕别人,内心才会平静,从容不迫。世上万物各有各的存在价值,每个人都是独特的个体,不必羡慕他人。

Chapter Fifty-Nine

Zhuang Zi's Wife Dies

ZHUANG ZI'S WIFE HAD JUST recently died. Huizi, who was Zhuang Zi's best friend, went to pay his respects to his dead wife. He saw that Zhuang Zi was squatting on the ground, knocking on the tile basin, and singing a song. Huizi was angry and said: 'Your wife has lived with you for many years, had your children and suffered a lot. Now she is dead, yet you don't cry for her but just sing a song, don't you think you are out of order?'

Zhuang Zi answered: 'It's not like that. When she died, was I not sad? After careful reflection, I realised that she originally had no life or form, not even a breath. Then she was born, she could breathe and took the form of a body, so she then had a life. Now a life turns back to death. This process of evolution is just like that – four seasons are a circle of change. I realised that she was sleeping in a big room within Heaven and Earth, but I was just crying beside her. This is when I understood that this is the process of the circle of life, so I stopped crying.'

庄子妻死

庄子的妻子死了，惠子前去吊丧，看见庄子蹲在地上，边敲瓦盆边唱着歌，惠子生气地说道："妻子跟你生活多年，替你生儿育女，跟你吃苦受罪，现在年老身死，你不哭倒也罢了，居然大唱起歌来，不太过分了吗？

庄子回答说："不是这样的。当她刚死的时候，我怎会不悲伤？可是仔细一观察，她原无生命；不但没有生命，而且也没有形体；非但没有形体，甚至连气息都没有。以后掺杂在恍恍惚惚若有若无的中间，才变化成有气息，有气息而有形体，有身体而有生命，现在再由生命变化成死亡。

"这种演变的过程，就像春夏秋冬四时的循环一样。想她此刻正安睡在天地的大房间里，我却在旁边哇哇地哭泣，实在是不明生命演变的过程，所以才停止了哭泣。"

Chapter Sixty

The Skeleton

Zhuang Zi saw a skeleton that had already dried up but was still formed. Zhuang Zi struck it with a whip and said: 'Were you killed because of cowardice, illegal behaviour, or murder? Maybe you died for the downfall of the nation? Or committed suicide for misbehaviour and were afraid of incriminating your family? For famine? For natural causes?'

After saying this, Zhuang Zi put the skeleton under his head and then fell asleep. In the middle of the night, Zhuang Zi dreamt that the skeleton said to him: 'What you talked about is the burden of a person alive, there are no such things after death. Do you want to hear about death?'

Zhuang Zi answered: 'Ok!', so the skeleton said: 'After death, there are no kings above or subjects below. No changes of the four seasons. The time passes calmly with the eternity of Heaven and Earth. Even the king's happiness cannot be compared with the present leisureliness.'

Zhuang Zi asked again: 'If I restore your flesh, return your life, and let you experience the joy of mankind, would you be willing to do so?' The skeleton refused because he was already used to the leisureliness of being with Heaven and Earth. How could he be happy if he returned to the disturbing world of mankind?

In the dialogue with the skeleton, all of Zhuang Zi's questions are applicable only to living people. What he wanted to express was the hopelessness of the obsession with life. We are alive and then we die, this is a necessary process for everyone. So why should we be happy about living or be sad for death? Uncertain and certain, life and death, these thoughts are the origin of all our trouble. The constant striving makes us too unable to find our true nature and therefore we suffer pain. We cannot control everything but living well in the moment is the most important principle.

骷髅

庄子看见一个骷髅，枯干了，但仍保有形状，于是，庄子拿着马鞭在上面敲了敲说："你是因为生前贪生怕死，行为不合法，被人杀死的呢?还是因为国破家亡被人害死的?是因为生前行为不好，怕连累父母妻儿受苦自杀的呢?还是穷困饥寒而死?或者是你寿品已尽，不得不死呢?"

说完这席话后，庄子把骷髅拿了过来，枕在头下睡了过去。到了半夜，庄子梦见骷髅向他说："刚才你谈话的神情，好像是士。至于你所说的内容，大多是活人的系累，死了就没有这些了。你想听听死后的情形吗?"

庄子答道："好啊!"骷说："死后，上面没有国君，下面没有臣子，也没有春夏秋冬四时的转变。从容安逸地把天地的长久看作是时令的流逝。即使帝王的快乐，也不可能超过现在的逍遥。"

当庄子再问骷髅："如果有法力让你恢复肉体，使你再世为人，体验人生的至乐，你可愿意？"骷髅拒绝了庄子的请求。看惯了山间清风与明月，那纷纷扰扰的世间还有什么至乐可言!

在与骷髅的对话中，庄子问的问题全部都是活在尘世的人们所受的拘累，他想表达的是对有待人生执念的无奈。真正的快乐又是什么呢？对快乐的追求，岂不是又一场执念在作祟吗？人生在世，生死轮回，何必为生而喜，为死而忧？无常与恒常，生与死，这些思考本都是烦恼的根源。人生之苦在于不断地向外求，不到自己的本来真性，然而我们无法把控一切，活好当下才更重要。

www.ingramcontent.com/pod-product-compliance
Lightning Source LLC
Chambersburg PA
CBHW071415160426
43195CB00013B/1698